Flexitarian Cookbook for Beginners

Flexitarian

COOKBOOK FOR BEGINNERS

QUICK AND EASY RECIPES FOR PLANT-BASED MEALS

Donna DeRosa

**ROCKRIDGE
PRESS**

Interior and Cover Designer: Jenny Paredes
Art Producer: Sara Feinstein
Editor: Kelly Koester
Production Editor: Rachel Taenzler
Production Manager: David Zapanta

Cover photography © 2022 Andrew Purcell. Cover food styling by Carrie Purcell. Interior photography © Marija Vidal, p. ii; Thomas J Story, p. vi, x, 35-36, 49; Andrew Purcell, p. viii; Elysa Weitala, p. 3, 6, 10, 14; Hélène Dujardin, p. 22, 64, 79-80; Annie Martin, p. 50; Tara Donne, p. 100, 110; Darren Muir, p. 120. Illustration used under license from Shutterstock.com.

Front cover: Kebabs with Spicy Peanut Sauce (page 89). Back cover, from top to bottom: Oatmeal-Raisin Breakfast Bowl (page 24), Hearty Chickpea Burgers (page 83), Seasonal Fruit Galette (page 108).

Paperback ISBN: 978-1-63878-208-7
eBook ISBN: 978-1-63878-704-4
R0

For Sam and Kitty,
with love.

CONTENTS

Introduction • *ix*

Chapter 1
A Flexible Guide to Eating Well • 1

Chapter 2
Breakfast • 23

Chapter 3
Vegetables and Sides • 37

Chapter 4
Salads and Handhelds • 51

Chapter 5
Soups and Stews • 65

Chapter 6
Entrées • 81

Chapter 7
Desserts • 101

Chapter 8
Sauces and Staples • 111

Measurement Conversions • 121

References • 122

Index • 124

INTRODUCTION

Welcome to the flexitarian diet.

The term "flexitarian" is simply a combination of the words "flexible" and "vegetarian." A flexitarian diet gives you the freedom to eat healthy plant-based foods most of the time and also enjoy meat and fish on occasion. For example, I eat primarily vegetarian meals, but on holidays like Thanksgiving, I don't want to miss out on turkey and the family traditions I remember so fondly. I also enjoy the occasional meatball with my pasta, and I try to eat fish once a week. My flexitarian lifestyle allows for all of this.

Plant-based diets are popular for their health benefits, and they're also kinder to the environment. If you are looking to live a more sustainable lifestyle and cut back on your meat consumption, a flexitarian diet can help you achieve those goals without eliminating whole food groups from your life. The health benefits from a plant-based diet may include weight loss and a reduced risk of heart disease, cancer, and type 2 diabetes. There are health benefits for our planet because we're reducing our carbon footprint by decreasing our meat consumption.

This book is designed to make it easy for you to try a flexitarian diet by offering simple, delicious recipes that use familiar ingredients you can find at any supermarket. I created these recipes to be quick and easy to make no matter how experienced you are in the kitchen.

There are two ways to benefit from this book: first, by using the recipes to eat mostly vegetables, fruits, beans, and whole grains, and only occasionally eat fish, meat, and dairy. Second, if your family is not interested in following a vegetarian or vegan lifestyle, you can change these plant-based meals to please everyone at the table. The book provides "Flex Tips" to show you how to adapt these plant-based recipes by adding red meat, poultry, fish, or dairy options.

The best part of a flexitarian diet is that it allows everyone to personalize their dining experience to their preferences and to suit their lifestyle. Enjoy! This is a judgment-free zone where everyone can make the diet decisions that feel right for them without complicating the cooking process.

CHAPTER 1

A Flexible Guide to Eating Well

Before we get to the recipes, let's go over the basic guidelines of a flexitarian diet. We'll cover what it means to eat flexitarian, the specifics about the types of foods you can eat, the health benefits of this lifestyle, and how to fit this new way of eating into your busy schedule.

The Principles of the Flexitarian Diet

The flexitarian diet has grown in popularity in recent years, but many people may be confused by the term "flexitarian" and wonder what exactly it means. Some refer to this way of eating as "semi-vegetarian." This style of eating has roots in ancient cultures and is very similar to the Mediterranean diet.

You can think of this diet in two ways: You want to live a primarily plant-based lifestyle, but you don't want to give up meat, fish, and dairy completely, or you want to adopt an entirely plant-based lifestyle, but your family is not on board and you want to offer them options.

Here are the diet's central tenets to consider:

Plant-Based: Fill your plate with mostly vegetables, fruits, grains, nuts, and seeds. Opt for minimally processed foods. Reduce your meat, fish, and dairy consumption. Allow some of these animal-based foods into your diet on occasion or create meals that are flexible to feed everyone in your family.

Vegetarian and Vegan: There are several types of vegetarians; some cut out meat completely but allow eggs and/or dairy. Vegans cut out anything from an animal. This choice means no meat, fish, dairy, or honey. Additionally, some vegans avoid buying animal products like leather.

Cooking Made Easy: All the recipes in this book are vegan, and most come with flexible options. They are quick and easy for beginners, with most taking less than 30 minutes to prepare and cook. They all use ingredients that are readily available at most supermarkets.

Inclusive Meals: A flexitarian diet means there is something on the menu for everyone. Each person holds their dietary needs in their own hands. You can create inclusive meal options by following the Flex Tips at the end of most recipes in this book.

Eating Close to the Earth: Eat seasonal vegetables and fruits grown as close to home as possible for maximum freshness and nutritional value.

Losing Weight vs. Gaining Health: Although you can certainly lose weight by eating a plant-based diet, consider it gaining health. The old saying "you are what you eat" really is true. The more plant-based foods you eat, the better you will feel.

Environmental Impact: When you reduce the use of animal products, your carbon footprint lowers significantly, which means you reduce your impact on the planet. In addition to improved health, this is one of the main reasons people adopt a flexitarian diet.

A Diet for Your Busy Lifestyle

A flexitarian lifestyle is ideal for people who don't want to spend all day in the kitchen prepping and cooking meals or those who are not veteran cooks. The recipes in this book are easy to follow, even for beginners. We all have busy lives, and I took that into account when writing this book. Why is a flexitarian diet so easy and convenient? Let's find out.

- Most recipes will take you 30 minutes or less, from start to finish.

- Most recipes are flexible and can be customized to suit the dietary needs of everyone at the table without a lot of hassle. There are plenty of flexitarian options throughout the book.

- When you're in a hurry, you can save time by using frozen vegetables. Frozen vegetables are packed at their peak freshness. Studies have shown frozen vegetables maintain more of their antioxidants than fresh vegetables stored in a refrigerator for three days.

- Canned beans are more convenient to use compared to dried, saving hours of prep time. They add substance to meals and are an excellent source of protein, fiber, and iron.

- Whole grains can be cooked in bulk and used throughout the week. They are high in dietary fiber, which helps you feel full and satisfied and makes it easier to maintain a healthy weight.

- Vegetables, fruits, beans, and whole grains are most often inexpensive ingredients, especially when compared to meat and seafood. Buying things locally and/or in season can also help cut costs and, if possible, so does buying in bulk.

The Health Benefits of a Flexitarian Diet

Adopting a primarily plant-based flexitarian lifestyle can impact your health in many positive ways. If you usually eat meat with every meal, you will be pleasantly surprised by the possible changes in your health.

Weight Management

Whole grains and vegetables are good sources of antioxidants and fiber, which are slower to digest and help prolong your feeling of fullness. This can help you eat less at meals and prevent snacking, so you consume fewer calories each day. Even if weight loss is not your main goal, studies show that people who consume high-quality plant-based foods find weight loss to be a by-product of this lifestyle. Plant eaters have a significantly lower body mass index (BMI) than meat eaters, thus lowering the risk of certain diseases.

Heart Health

According to the *Journal of the American College of Cardiology*, people who eat fewer animal products and embrace a primarily plant-based diet can lower their level of "bad" cholesterol, or LDL (low-density lipoprotein), by 10 to 15 percent. Cholesterol is a waxy substance that can build up in your blood vessels and prevent blood flow. Lowering your LDL can reduce your risk of developing cardiovascular disease.

Saturated fats, found in red meat, poultry, butter, cream, and milk, can raise LDL. Eating foods rich in fiber and omega-3 fatty acids, such as whole grains, fruits, vegetables, and fish, can reduce LDL while increasing HDL (high-density lipoprotein), the "good" cholesterol.

Diabetes

PLoS Medicine, a peer-reviewed medical journal, analyzed three studies of more than 200,000 people to determine if a plant-based diet can affect the risk of developing type 2 diabetes. It found a diet that emphasized plant-based foods and lowered animal food intake could reduce the risk of type 2 diabetes by 20 percent.

The reduction in risk of developing type 2 diabetes improved to 34 percent if people consumed plant foods like high-quality grains, vegetables, beans, nuts, and seeds rather than sugary, refined, and overly processed plant-based foods. There is a direct link between diet and type 2 diabetes.

Cancer Prevention

The American Institute for Cancer Research says the best way to protect your cells from damage is to ingest nutrients such as dietary fiber, minerals, and phytochemicals. These can be found in a diet rich in fruits, vegetables, grains, beans, nuts, seeds, and a small amount of animal products.

According to the Mayo Clinic, eating lots of fruits, vegetables, and legumes and little to no meat or other animal products can help prevent one-third of cancer cases.

Other Benefits

Multiple studies have also shown a plant-based diet can reduce inflammation, improve kidney function and gut health, and lower the risk for strokes, developing high blood pressure, and cognitive decline.

As you can see, a flexitarian diet has many benefits. Not only are the foods delicious, but they also nourish your body in a way that protects your cells and helps prevent multiple diseases.

Environmental Impact

According to the British scientific journal *Nature*, our global food system has a major impact on climate change. It estimates that if we continue to use the land and our freshwater resources at our current levels of agricultural production, by the year 2050, our planet will be beyond the boundaries "that define a safe operating system for humanity."

To put it simply, we damage the environment and use up our natural resources by growing food because about half of the grain we grow on this planet is fed to the animals we eat. If we consume fewer animal products, we can eat the plant-based products ourselves and lessen the impact on the planet.

The researchers analyzed the effects of adopting a vegan or flexitarian lifestyle to impact our environment positively. Although adopting a vegan lifestyle can significantly improve our impact on the planet, it may not be easy for everyone in the world to maintain. Adopting a flexitarian diet is easier and more palatable for most people and can still contribute to a significant positive impact on climate change.

Although most of us are interested in gaining health through a flexitarian diet, another positive side effect is helping nurture and save our planet, which feeds us these beautiful, nutritious foods.

To start this lifestyle, ease into it. When grocery shopping, substitute portobello mushrooms for steak, beans for ground beef, nut milk for cow's milk. These simple acts can open a whole new world for you.

Core Plant-Based Proteins

For most people, the hardest adjustment when adopting a flexitarian diet is replacing animal proteins with plant-based proteins. But don't worry, there are plenty of tasty protein sources in the plant world.

The Recommended Dietary Allowance (RDA) for protein is about 10 percent of your daily caloric intake. You should have no problem meeting that minimum requirement. You'll also save money because these ingredients cost less than meat.

Beans and Legumes

Beans and legumes are the edible seeds and pods of plants such as peas, lentils, and various beans. They are an excellent plant-based protein replacement for meat. They are also rich in fiber and B vitamins. Health benefits include reducing cholesterol, increasing healthy gut bacteria, and managing blood sugar levels.

High-protein choices are chickpeas, lentils, peas, kidney beans, cannellini beans, lima beans, black beans, soybeans, pinto beans, and peanuts. Yes, peanuts are a legume, not a nut. Add them to soups, stews, and salads, or as a side dish to your vegetables.

Tofu, Tempeh, and Other Soy Products

Soybeans are high in protein and are made into various food products such as tofu, tempeh, soy milk, and soy protein powder.

Tofu—also known as bean curd—is made by coagulating soy milk and pressing it into solid white blocks. The texture choices include silken, soft, and firm, and it has a neutral flavor. Tempeh is made by fermenting soybeans and binding them into a cake form. It has a chewy texture and nutty flavor.

Both adapt well to the flavors of the food and can be a welcome replacement for meat.

Nuts and Seeds

Nuts and seeds are versatile and portable. You can add them to meals as a delicious source of protein or carry them with you for an on-the-go snack. They are excellent sources of plant-based protein. Sprinkle them on salads and soups, add them to smoothies and baked goods, or eat them by themselves.

Choices include walnuts, pistachios, cashews, almonds, pine nuts, Brazil nuts, hazelnuts, pumpkin seeds, chia seeds, sunflower seeds, sesame seeds, and ground flaxseed. According to the Mayo Clinic, nuts and seeds are a good source of healthy fats and can help lower cholesterol and triglyceride levels and improve your arteries' linings.

High-Protein Vegetables

Vegetables are the key to a plant-based diet. Try to eat 5 to 10 servings of vegetables a day in a variety of colors. Each color will provide you with different necessary nutrients. Make sure at least one of them is a dark leafy green.

Although all vegetables are good for you, some offer more protein than others. Did you know that broccoli contains more protein per calorie than steak, and spinach is equal to chicken and fish? Other high-protein choices are cauliflower, Brussels sprouts, corn, potatoes, sweet potatoes, asparagus, avocados, artichokes, mushrooms, watercress, cabbage, bok choy, mustard greens, and collard greens.

Flexitarian Essentials for Beginners

Besides the plant-based proteins found in vegetables, beans, and nuts, you also need a variety of essential vitamins and minerals every day, as well as a variety of flavors and textures to keep you satisfied. Here are some more food categories that are essential to a healthy flexitarian diet.

Fruit

Fruits are a great source of vitamins, minerals, and fiber. They are hydrating and offer a variety of antioxidants. A diet rich in fruits and vegetables can reduce the risk of developing heart disease, cancer, inflammation, and diabetes.

Try incorporating a variety of fruits into your meals, such as apples, blueberries, bananas, lemons, oranges, mango, avocado, pineapple, strawberries, cherries, olives, watermelon, kiwi, peaches, and grapes. Add fruit to salads or smoothies or eat them plain for dessert and snacks.

Greens

Leafy greens are nutrient-dense and low calorie. Add them to sandwiches and smoothies, toss a handful into salads, cook them in soups, stews, and pasta dishes, or enjoy them as a side dish.

The top greens for nutrient density are watercress, Swiss chard, mustard greens, dandelion greens, turnip tops, collard greens, beet greens, spinach, broccoli rabe, cabbage, and the many types of kale. They range in taste from mild to peppery and add wonderful flavor, nutrients, and texture to your meals.

Eating a diet rich in leafy greens can help reduce the risk of heart disease, hypertension, and cognitive decline. Aim to eat at least one serving of dark leafy greens every day.

Whole Grains

Whole grains offer nutrients such as protein, fiber, B vitamins, antioxidants, and iron. They also support healthy digestion and are a good source of complex carbohydrates. Adding different whole grains to your diet can reduce the risk of heart disease, stroke, type 2 diabetes, obesity, and some forms of cancer.

Grains add substance to your meals and help you feel full. They come in various textures and nutty flavors. Try whole oats, bread made of whole wheat and rye, farro, buckwheat, bulgar, millet, barley, spelt, quinoa (which is a pseudograin), brown and wild rice, and corn.

The Flexitarian Approach to Cooking with Meat, Eggs, and Dairy

All the recipes in this book are vegan. Some were adapted from familiar favorite meals and given a plant-based makeover, but you can easily convert them back.

When you follow a flexitarian diet, most of your meals should be vegan or vegetarian. Meat, dairy, and eggs are an occasional side dish or incorporated into meals in small quantities. When building your meals, fill half of your plate with vegetables, a quarter with a whole grain, and the last quarter with beans, fruit, or a small serving of meat, dairy, or eggs.

When you want to eat animal products, think of them as side dishes or toppings rather than the focus of the meal. Portion sizes should be 3 to 4 ounces at most, or half of that amount if you can. Sometimes just a taste can satisfy a craving.

Cook with the highest quality ingredients you can find and afford. If possible, buy organic eggs and dairy, and grass-fed lean cuts of beef or poultry. Don't stress about it too much if you can't find organic. Keep pork and ham as a flavor enhancer, like adding a little pancetta or bacon to a dish.

When cooking flexitarian, you can make a vegan-based dish and, in a separate pan, prepare meat, eggs, or dairy for the rest of the family. Or you can add them directly to the main dish if you desire. Most recipes in this book have "Flex Tips" recommending ways to do this.

For example, traditional shakshuka is made by cooking eggs in a tomato-based sauce. My recipe (see page 34) uses avocado halves instead, or toasted polenta. You can make eggs on the side for those who want them or add the eggs back to the recipe for everyone to enjoy.

Have fun with it and be creative.

Flex-Friendly Fish and Seafood

Fish and seafood can be a side dish or added directly to a recipe on occasion. For example, it's very easy to grill or sauté a few shrimp on the side for those who want a pescatarian meal. Shrimp, mussels, clams, or a can of tuna are easy additions to pasta dishes or salads.

Healthy fish choices include salmon, tuna, mackerel, trout, herring, and sardines. These oily, fatty fishes are high in omega-3 fatty acids, which are good for your heart, lungs, and blood vessels. They can also help reduce inflammation in the body and improve brain function.

Other, leaner fish like cod, flounder, mahi-mahi, halibut, and catfish have lower levels of omega-3s but are healthy sources of protein, B vitamins, and other important nutrients. They are quick and easy to prepare and make an excellent addition to dishes like Family-Style Taco Bar (page 63).

Don't shy away from canned or frozen seafood, either. I often buy frozen, shelled shrimp; they defrost and cook up in a few minutes. I also enjoy canned tuna, mackerel, sardines, and anchovies. Tuna mixed with a little mayo is a great sandwich filler. Canned mackerel, sardines, and anchovies are wonderful in salads and pasta dishes.

Shellfish like mussels and clams are best fresh and eaten the same day. They cook up quickly and make an excellent appetizer course or a tasty addition to pasta dishes.

Stocking the Flexitarian Kitchen

Here are some ingredients and tools to have on hand for preparing the recipes.

Fridge and Freezer Staples

Stock your refrigerator and freezer with these flexitarian staples:

- Avocados
- Condiments (Dijon mustard, vegan mayo, hot pepper relish)
- Dark leafy greens
- Eggs (optional)
- Fresh herbs (basil, thyme, rosemary, parsley, chives, sage)
- Fresh vegetables (celery, carrots, cucumbers, mushrooms, tomatoes)
- Frozen shrimp (optional)
- Frozen spinach and mixed vegetables (with no added sauces or seasonings)
- Fruit (lemons, limes, oranges, apples, bananas, pears, and berries)
- Plant-based milk
- Shallots, onions, scallions, garlic, olives

Pantry Staples

You may have many of these ingredients in your pantry already, so double-check before buying anything.

- Bread (whole wheat, rye, sourdough, French baguette)
- Canned beans (cannellini, black, pinto, chickpeas)
- Canned tuna
- Crushed tomatoes (canned, low sodium)
- Dried herbs (oregano, salt, black pepper, garlic powder, red pepper flakes)
- Dried lentils
- Nuts and seeds
- Olive oil (extra-virgin)
- Root vegetables (potatoes, sweet potatoes, carrots, turnips)
- Semolina pasta (most are egg-free) (couscous, spaghetti, lasagna shells, orzo, various shapes)
- Whole grains (oatmeal, farro, quinoa, rice, polenta)

Tools and Equipment

The recipes in this book require some common kitchen tools, but nothing expensive or difficult to find.

- Baking dishes. For casseroles and other baked dishes (small 2-quart and large 3-quart).

- Baking sheets, rimmed. For baking cookies and roasting vegetables.
- Braising pan. This is a heavy-duty cast-iron pan with an enamel coating that goes from stovetop to oven.
- Cutting boards. For prepping ingredients, including chopping vegetables and fruits.
- Dutch oven. This is a heavy-duty pot typically used for soups and stews.
- Food processor. For quick chopping and pureeing.
- Parchment paper or aluminum foil. For lining sheet pans, cooking fish, covering baking dishes, and more.
- Pie pans (9-inch). For entrées and desserts.
- Saucepans and skillets. These come in various sizes and various materials.
- Storage containers. Glass, in various sizes with lids.

The Keys to Flexitarian Cooking

Although the recipes in this flexitarian cookbook are designed for beginner cooks, there are some ways to make them even easier. Think about your lifestyle and how much time you devote to cooking each day. On some days you may have more time than others. Use the following tips to save time shopping, prepping, and cooking.

Create Weekly Meal Plans: A little forethought and a weekly plan will save you time while shopping and help you stick to your budget. Map out your meals in advance, so you always know what is on the menu.

Write Shopping Lists: Always go shopping with a list in hand to help keep you on budget and not forget any ingredients. Write the list with the store's layout in mind, so you can go from aisle to aisle without running around.

Food Preparation: If you pre-chop vegetables, precook whole grains, roast a baking sheet full of vegetables, or make a batch of tomato sauce, you can pull together meals in a matter of minutes. Set aside one day of the week to prepare your ingredients to mix and match into quick, nutritious meals.

Use Frozen Vegetables: When pressed for time, it's nice to know you have a bag of pre-chopped vegetables in the freezer, so you don't have to go shopping at the last minute. They also cook quickly. Throw them into soups or stews, or sauté them and serve over rice or the whole grain of your choice.

Batch Cook and Freeze: Cook more portions of meals and freeze them for another time. This works especially well with soups, stews, and tomato sauces. You can also freeze fresh bread and thaw it out in the refrigerator on the day you want to use it.

Reinvent Leftovers: Don't know what to do with leftover risotto? Use it to stuff peppers or add to wraps. Have leftover stew? Reheat it and toss with pasta or serve it over rice for a completely different meal. Get creative!

Invest in Kitchen Tools: A food processor, garlic press, chef's knife, mandoline, or stick blender, although not necessary, can save time in the kitchen. Food processors chop vegetables in seconds. A mandoline creates perfectly thin slices of vegetables. A stick blender purees soups and sauces in minutes. Look for practical tools that save you time.

Getting Started with Meal Planning

Planning meals in advance saves time in the kitchen and helps keep you on budget when shopping. You won't come home after a busy day and stress about what to put on the table.

In this book I have included two weeklong meal plans. They will help you ease into a more plant-based lifestyle with easy flexible options for people who are used to consuming meat, fish, and poultry regularly. All the recipes in the meal plans are included in this book along with flexitarian options.

The first meal plan features plant-based meals with options for flexing with poultry and seafood. The second offers meatless meals with options for flexing with eggs and dairy.

I've designed these meals to be easy to make and to use ingredients that are readily available. Some can be made in advance, and some can be reused as leftovers later in the week. That's the way I eat at home, and I think it will benefit you to learn these tips, too.

For example, at the start of the week I like to roast a large sheet pan of vegetables, and throughout the week I toss them in pasta, or serve them over whole grains, or add them to broth for soup. I also make a big pot of whole grains for hot breakfasts or side dishes. I choose a new grain each week. I mix and match these ingredients in creative ways to make unique meals. This way I can have nutritious meals on the table in 30 minutes or less.

Five Fast Flex Favorites

All the recipes in this book are easy to prepare, but a few stand out as especially quick. Here are five favorites inspired by cuisines around the world:

◆ **GLT Sandwich** (page 33): It takes 10 minutes to make the guacamole, toast the sourdough, slice the tomatoes and lettuce, and assemble. I included this recipe in the breakfast chapter, but this sandwich is tasty any time of day.

◆ **Nouveau Greek Salad** (page 59): You can make the vinaigrette in 2 minutes or less. The rest is just chopping the fresh ingredients and tossing them in a bowl.

◆ **Easy Gazpacho** (page 78): Gazpacho is almost effortless. Pulse all the ingredients in a blender and serve garnished with chopped vegetables. Serve in a fancy glass if you feel festive.

◆ **Spaghetti with Olive Oil, Garlic, and Olives** (page 93): This meal comes together in the time it takes to boil the pasta, which is usually 9 to 11 minutes. You can prepare the other ingredients while the pasta cooks.

◆ **Egg-Roll-in-a-Bowl Stir-Fry** (page 86): This dish takes 20 minutes. It includes a plant-based protein and can be jazzed up with some crunchy vegetables near the end. Serve in lettuce cups for a fun presentation.

EXAMPLE WEEK 1: FLEXING WITH POULTRY AND SEAFOOD

DAY	BREAKFAST	LUNCH	DINNER	SNACK
DAY 1	Zucchini-Carrot Oatmeal Muffins (page 27)	Chopped Avocado Chickpea Salad with Olives (page 53)	Flex Meal: Red Curry Vegetables plus Flex Tip (page 85)	Hummus (page 116) with carrot sticks
DAY 2	Mushroom and Scallion Chickpea Omelet (page 28)	*Leftovers: Red Curry Vegetables plus Flex Tip*	Flex Meal: Pizza Pockets plus Flex Tip (page 57)	¼ cup of almonds
DAY 3	Pear and Farro Bowl (page 30)	*Leftovers: Pizza Pockets*	Flex Meal: Kebabs with Spicy Peanut Sauce plus Flex Tip (page 89)	*Leftovers: 1 Zucchini-Carrot Oatmeal Muffin*
DAY 4	*Leftovers: Zucchini-Carrot Oatmeal Muffins*	*Leftovers: Kebabs with Spicy Peanut Sauce*	Flex Meal: Classic Vegetable Soup with Flex Tip (page 66)	1 pear
DAY 5	*Leftovers: Pear and Farro Bowl*	Salad with Peach Carpaccio (page 58)	Flex Meal: Family-Style Taco Bar with Flex Tip (page 63)	Roasted Jalapeño and Lime Guacamole with pita bread (page 114)
DAY 6	Berry Blast Smoothie Bowl (page 31)	*Leftovers: Family-Style Taco Bar with Flex Tip*	Easy Ratatouille (page 45)	1 peach
DAY 7	Polenta with Potato and Red Onion (page 32)	Nouveau Greek Salad (page 59)	Gnocchi Puttanesca (page 91)	¼ cup of almonds

SHOPPING LIST

PRODUCE

- Avocado (2)
- Banana (1 bunch)
- Basil (1 bunch)
- Bell pepper, green (4)
- Bell pepper, red (4)
- Bell pepper, orange (1)
- Cabbage, green (1 head)
- Carrots (1 pound)
- Celery (1 stalk)
- Cilantro (1 bunch)
- Cucumber (2)
- Eggplant (2)
- Garlic (4 heads)
- Ginger (4-inch piece)
- Green beans (1 cup)
- Jalapeño peppers (2 to 6)

- Lemons (7)
- Lettuce, mixed greens (6 cups or 7¼ ounces)
- Limes (4)
- Mushrooms (4 cups)
- Onions, red (4)
- Onions, yellow (11)
- Peaches (3)
- Pears (5)
- Potatoes, russet (3 large)
- Radishes (4)
- Scallions (1 bunch)
- Spinach, baby (4 cups or 4¼ ounces)
- Tomatoes, cherry or grape (2 pints)
- Tomatoes (6)
- Yellow squash (1)
- Zucchini (6)

DAIRY, NONDAIRY ALTERNATIVES, AND EGGS

- Cheese, vegan, mozzarella-style, shredded (½ cup)
- Egg (1)
- Milk, almond, unsweetened (1 quart)
- Milk, almond, unsweetened vanilla (1 pint)

POULTRY AND SEAFOOD

- Chicken, 1 pound ground
- Chicken, 1 pound boneless, skinless breasts
- Shrimp, 1 pound medium ($^{40}/_{50}$ count), peeled and deveined

FROZEN

- Banana slices (1 cup)
- Berries, mixed (2 cups)
- Vegetables, stir-fry, 1 (16-ounce) bag

HERBS AND SPICES

- Basil, dried (2 teaspoons)
- Bay leaf (2)
- Black pepper, freshly ground
- Chili powder (1 teaspoon)
- Cinnamon, ground (½ teaspoon)
- Cumin, ground (½ teaspoon)
- Garlic powder (2 teaspoons)
- Herbes de Provence (1 tablespoon)
- Italian seasoning (1 tablespoon)
- Mint, dried (½ teaspoon)
- Onion powder (¼ teaspoon)
- Oregano, dried (5 teaspoons)

- Paprika, smoked (1 teaspoon)
- Parsley, dried (1 teaspoon)
- Red pepper flakes (½ teaspoon)
- Salt
- Thyme, dried (½ teaspoon)

PANTRY

- Almonds, whole (½ cup)
- Applesauce, unsweetened 1 (24-ounce) jar
- Baking powder
- Beans, black, 1 (15-ounce) can
- Beans, butter, 1 (15-ounce) can
- Beans, pinto, 1 (15-ounce) can
- Bread crumbs (1 container)
- Capers, 1 (2-ounce) jar
- Chickpeas, 2 (15-ounce) cans
- Chili paste, Calabrian (1 teaspoon)
- Coconut flakes
- Cornstarch
- Curry paste, Thai red (1 tablespoon)
- Farro, pearled (1 cup)
- Flaxseed, ground (¼ cup)
- Flour, all-purpose (1½ cups)
- Flour, chickpea (1 cup)
- Gnocchi, 1 (17-ounce) package
- Jalapeño peppers, pickled, 1 (12-ounce) jar
- Maple syrup, 1 (12-ounce) bottle
- Milk, coconut, full-fat, 1 (13½-ounce) can
- Miso paste, red (1 tablespoon)
- Oats, old-fashioned (½ cup)
- Oil, olive, extra-virgin, 1 (25-ounce) bottle
- Olives, Kalamata, 1 (12-ounce) jar
- Peanut butter, 1 (16-ounce) jar
- Pepperoncini, pickled, 1 (16-ounce) jar
- Polenta, instant (1½ cups)
- Pumpkin seeds
- Sugar, granulated (½ cup)
- Tahini (¼ cup)
- Tomatoes, crushed, 2 (28-ounce) cans
- Tomatoes, diced, 1 (28-ounce) can
- Vanilla extract (2 teaspoons)
- Vinegar, red wine, 1 (16-ounce) jar
- Vinegar, white wine, 1 (16-ounce) jar
- Walnuts, raw (1 cup)

OTHER

- Granola
- Nutritional yeast (⅓ cup)
- Pizza dough, 1 (1-pound) ball
- Tortillas, vegan (selection of soft and hard)

EXAMPLE WEEK 2: MEATLESS FLEXING WITH DAIRY AND EGGS

DAY	BREAKFAST	LUNCH	DINNER	SNACK
DAY 1	Oatmeal-Raisin Breakfast Bowl (page 24)	Root Vegetable Soup (page 68)	Flex Meal: Vegan Lasagna plus Flex Tip (page 87)	¼ cup almonds
DAY 2	*Leftovers: Oatmeal-Raisin Breakfast Bowl*	*Leftovers: Vegan Lasagna plus Flex Tip*	Southwest Stuffed Peppers (page 82)	Root Vegetable Chips (page 48)
DAY 3	Veggie and White Bean Scramble (page 29)	*Leftovers: Southwest Stuffed Peppers*	Flex Meal: Burst Cherry Tomato Rigatoni plus Flex Tip (page 84)	¼ cup of berries
DAY 4	*Leftovers: Veggie and White Bean Scramble*	*Leftovers: Burst Cherry Tomato Rigatoni plus Flex Tip*	Flex Meal: Spinach Orzo Soup plus Flex Tip (page 75)	1 apple
DAY 5	Tropical Smoothie Bowl (page 31)	*Leftovers: Spinach Orzo Soup plus Flex Tip*	Flex Meal: Coconut Curry Ramen plus Flex Tip (page 70)	*Leftovers: Root Vegetable Chips*
DAY 6	*Leftovers: Tropical Smoothie Bowl*	*Leftovers: Coconut Curry Ramen plus Flex Tip*	Vegetable Paella (page 96)	1 pear
DAY 7	Whole Wheat Pancakes (page 26)	*Leftovers: Vegetable Paella*	Flex Meal: Green Shakshuka plus Flex Tip (page 34)	¼ cup of almonds

SHOPPING LIST

PRODUCE

- Apple (1)
- Avocado (2)
- Banana (1 bunch)
- Basil (2 bunches)
- Bell pepper, green (5)
- Bell pepper, red (2)
- Berries, your choice (1 cup)
- Bok choy, baby (2 heads)

- Broccoli (1 bunch)
- Cabbage, red (1 head)
- Carrots (1 pound)
- Celery (1 stalk)
- Garlic (3 heads)
- Ginger (4-inch piece)
- Green beans (1 cup)
- Kiwi (1)

- Leeks (2)
- Lemons (1)
- Lettuce, iceberg (1 head)
- Limes (1)
- Mushrooms, cremini (6)
- Mushrooms, portobello (4)
- Onions, yellow (5)
- Parsley (1 bunch)
- Parsnip (1)
- Pear (1)
- Peas, snow (1 cup)
- Potato, russet (1 large)
- Potatoes, sweet (3)
- Root vegetables, your choice (4)
- Spinach, baby (7 cups or 8 ounces)
- Thyme (1 bunch)
- Tomatoes, cherry or grape (1 pint)
- Tomato (1)
- Turnip (1)
- Yellow squash (1)
- Zucchini (1)

DAIRY, NONDAIRY ALTERNATIVES, AND EGGS

- Butter, vegan (¼ cup)
- Cheese, Parmesan (3 tablespoons)
- Cheese, Italian blend (1 cup)
- Eggs (8)
- Milk, plant-based, unsweetened (5½ cups)

FROZEN

- Corn (1 cup)
- Mango, chunks (½ cup)
- Peas (1½ cups)
- Pineapple, chunks (½ cup)
- Spinach, baby (1 cup)

HERBS AND SPICES

- Basil, dried (½ teaspoon)
- Black pepper, freshly ground
- Cayenne pepper (½ teaspoon)
- Chili powder (2 tablespoons)
- Cinnamon, ground (2 teaspoons)
- Cumin, ground (1 teaspoon)
- Garlic powder (½ teaspoon)
- Ginger, ground (½ teaspoon)
- Nutmeg
- Onion powder (½ teaspoon)
- Oregano, dried (3 tablespoons)
- Red pepper flakes (3 teaspoons)
- Salt

PANTRY

- Almonds, whole (½ cup)
- Baking powder (2 tablespoons)
- Beans, black, 1 (15-ounce) can
- Beans, cannellini, 2 (19-ounce) cans
- Chickpeas, 1 (15-ounce) can
- Coconut flakes
- Coconut water (¼ cup)
- Curry paste, Thai red (2 or 3 tablespoons)
- Dates, pitted (¼ cup)
- Flaxseed, ground (3 tablespoons)
- Flour, all-purpose (⅓ cup)
- Flour, rye (½ cup)
- Flour, whole wheat pastry (1½ cups)
- Maple syrup, 1 (12-ounce) bottle
- Milk, coconut, full-fat, 1 (13 ½-ounce) can
- Oats, steel-cut (1 cup)
- Oil, olive, extra-virgin, 1 (25-ounce) bottle
- Olives, Kalamata, 1 (12-ounce) jar
- Orzo (1½ cups)
- Pecans, chopped (¼ cup)
- Raisins (½ cup)
- Rice, brown (1½ cups)
- Rice, Arborio (1 cup)
- Rigatoni, whole wheat, 1 (16-ounce) box
- Tomatoes, crushed, 2 (28-ounce) cans
- Tomatoes, fire-roasted, diced, 1 (14½-ounce) can
- Tomatoes, whole cherry, 3 (14-ounce) cans
- Tomato paste, 2 (6-ounce) cans
- Vanilla extract (2 teaspoons)

OTHER

- Bread, pita (1 package)
- Bread, sourdough (8 slices)
- Granola
- Noodles, instant ramen, 4 (3-ounce) packages
- Tortellini, cheese, 1 (16-ounce) package
- Wine, white, dry (¼ cup)

The Recipes in This Book

All the recipes in this flexitarian cookbook are vegan, with many of them offering tips for making flexible meals by adding dairy, meat, eggs, fish, or seafood when desired. The recipe chapters include breakfast, vegetables, side dishes, salads, soups, sandwiches, complete entrées, desserts, sauces, and everything in between.

Most of the healthy dishes in this book serve 4 to 6 people. They are easy enough for beginners, as the title suggests. Each recipe contains one or more of the following labels:

5/FEWER ING. **5 or Fewer Ingredients**: The recipe has 5 ingredients or less, excluding "freebies" like salt, pepper, and oil/cooking spray.

FAST FAV. **Fast Favorite**: The recipe is made and ready in 30 minutes or less.

ONE-POT **One-Pot Meal**: The recipe is made entirely in one pot or pan.

 Quick Prep: The recipe takes 5 minutes or less to prep.

The 75 recipes in this book will help you ease into the flexitarian lifestyle by offering delicious plant-based recipes, and the majority have options for adding small amounts of dairy or animal proteins in whatever ways work for you. Many other recipes include tips for ways to cut down on prep or cooking times, suggestions to adjust the flavor or texture with an added ingredient, and/or advice on leftover storage and meal plating. You will find meals in this book that satisfy you and your whole family.

Take your health into your own hands and into your own kitchen. Create meals that please everyone at your table without a lot of fuss and drama. Each person can make their own decisions about the foods suitable for them while enjoying a family meal.

I truly hope this book inspires you to eat a predominantly plant-based diet without sacrificing flavor or spending a lot of time doing busy work.

I wish you many happy meals in the years to come!

Mushroom and Scallion Chickpea Omelet ◆ 28

CHAPTER 2

Breakfast

Oatmeal-Raisin Breakfast Bowl ◆ 24

Carrot Cake Oatmeal ◆ 25

Whole Wheat Pancakes ◆ 26

Zucchini-Carrot Oatmeal Muffins ◆ 27

Mushroom and Scallion Chickpea Omelet ◆ 28

Veggie and White Bean Scramble ◆ 29

Pear and Farro Bowl ◆ 30

Smoothie Bowls, 3 Ways ◆ 31

Polenta with Potato and Red Onion ◆ 32

GLT Sandwich ◆ 33

Green Shakshuka ◆ 34

Oatmeal-Raisin Breakfast Bowl

FAST FAV. | ONE-POT | QUICK PREP.

SERVES: 4 | **PREP TIME:** 5 MINUTES | **COOK TIME:** 25 MINUTES

Oatmeal may seem like a more traditional breakfast, but this recipe smells like cookies. Cooking these oats with plant-based milk creates a creamy texture. Oatmeal is already easy to cook, but using an Instant Pot or another multicooker with a pressure-cooking function makes it even easier and quicker. Just increase the plant-based milk to 3 cups, cook on high pressure for 5 minutes, then use a natural pressure release.

2 cups unsweetened
plant-based milk
1 cup steel-cut oats

½ cup raisins
1 teaspoon ground
cinnamon

¼ cup chopped pitted dates
¼ cup chopped pecans

1. In a large saucepan, combine the milk, oats, raisins, and cinnamon, and bring to a boil over medium-high heat.

2. Lower the heat to low and simmer, stirring occasionally, until the oats are tender, about 25 minutes.

3. Remove from the heat. Stir in the dates and pecans and serve.

> **TIP:** Feel free to use dairy milk instead of the plant-based milk. To make this nut-free, try sunflower seeds instead. You can also replace the dates with any other dried fruit or even cacao nibs or shredded coconut.

PER SERVING: Calories: 355; Fat: 9g; Protein: 9g; Carbohydrates: 61g, Fiber: 7g; Sugar: 20g; Sodium: 64mg

Carrot Cake Oatmeal

FAST FAV.

SERVES: 2 | **PREP TIME:** 10 MINUTES | **COOK TIME:** 15 MINUTES

Including shredded carrot in your morning oatmeal boosts nutrition and adds plant-based fiber. The simple combination of familiar spices makes this hearty bowl a decadent treat, and the cinnamon helps curb cravings throughout your morning by controlling blood sugar levels. Top your carrot cake oats with fresh fruit, nut butters, and seeds to make it even more hearty and nutritious. Quick oats and certified gluten-free oats will give similar results.

¼ cup pecans

1¼ cups unsweetened nondairy milk

1 cup finely shredded carrot

½ cup old-fashioned oats

1 tablespoon pure maple syrup

1 teaspoon ground cinnamon

1 teaspoon ground ginger

¼ teaspoon ground nutmeg

2 tablespoons chia seeds

1. In a small skillet over medium-high heat, toast the pecans for 3 to 4 minutes, stirring often, until browned and fragrant (watch closely, as they can burn quickly). Pour the pecans onto a cutting board and coarsely chop them. Set aside.

2. In an 8-quart pot over medium-high heat, combine the milk, carrot, oats, maple syrup, cinnamon, ginger, and nutmeg. Bring to a boil, then reduce the heat to medium-low. Cook, uncovered, for 10 minutes, stirring occasionally.

3. Stir in the chopped pecans and chia seeds. Serve immediately.

> **TIP:** The oatmeal can also be prepared by mixing all the ingredients in a sealable container and refrigerating overnight. The texture will be chewier and denser, but overnight oats are an easy meal prep for a quick breakfast.

PER SERVING: Calories: 307; Fat: 17g; Protein: 13g; Carbohydrates: 35g, Fiber: 11g; Sugar: 10g; Sodium: 96mg

Whole Wheat Pancakes

FAST FAV.

SERVES: 4 | **PREP TIME:** 10 MINUTES | **COOK TIME:** 20 MINUTES

Most egg-free pancakes rely on bananas or applesauce, but these heavier-binding ingredients make pancakes tough and rubbery. Flaxseed meal, or ground flaxseed, acts as the egg replacer here and adds necessary omega-3 fatty acids. Top your pancakes with date syrup, fresh fruit, and nut butter to make them even more filling and nutritious.

3 tablespoons ground flaxseed

6 tablespoons warm water

1½ cups whole wheat pastry flour

½ cup rye flour

2 tablespoons double-acting baking powder

1 teaspoon ground cinnamon

½ teaspoon ground ginger

1½ cups unsweetened nondairy milk

3 tablespoons pure maple syrup

1 teaspoon vanilla extract

1. In a small bowl, stir together the flaxseed and warm water. Set aside for at least 5 minutes.

2. In a large bowl, whisk together the pastry and rye flours, baking powder, cinnamon, and ginger to combine.

3. In a glass measuring cup, whisk together the milk, maple syrup, and vanilla. Using a spatula, fold the wet ingredients into the dry ingredients. Fold in the soaked flaxseed until fully incorporated.

4. Heat a large skillet or nonstick griddle over medium-high heat. Working in batches, 3 to 4 pancakes at a time, add ¼-cup portions of batter to the hot skillet. Cook for 3 to 4 minutes per side, or until golden brown and no liquid batter is visible.

TIP: Any whole wheat flour will work here, but the best grind for lightly baked goods is the pastry variety. Non-pastry grinds have sharper pieces of bran, which can form air pockets and make your baked goods flat.

PER SERVING (3 PANCAKES): Calories: 301; Fat: 4g; Protein: 11g; Carbohydrates: 57g; Fiber: 10g; Sugar: 10g; Sodium: 581mg

Zucchini-Carrot Oatmeal Muffins

(FAST FAV.)

MAKES: 12 MUFFINS | **PREP TIME:** 10 MINUTES | **COOK TIME:** 20 MINUTES

This recipe sneaks some veggies into the batter. Kids will think they are eating a delicious treat, but you'll know they're also getting a serving of veggies. This recipe uses flaxseed and applesauce as binders, adding extra fiber and vitamin C, and keeping these muffins oil-free.

1½ cups all-purpose flour
½ cup old-fashioned oats
½ cup sugar
1 tablespoon baking powder
¼ teaspoon salt

¼ cup hot water
2 tablespoons ground flaxseed
1 cup unsweetened almond milk

1 cup grated zucchini
1 cup shredded carrots
¼ cup unsweetened applesauce

1. Preheat the oven to 350°F. Line a standard muffin tin with paper liners or grease well.

2. In a large bowl, combine the flour, oats, sugar, baking powder, and salt.

3. In a medium bowl, whisk together the hot water and flaxseed, then add the almond milk, zucchini, carrots, and applesauce. Whisk to combine.

4. Pour the wet mixture into the dry mixture and stir until just combined and no flour streaks are left behind.

5. Using a 2-inch ice cream scoop (or a ¼-cup measuring cup), evenly divide the batter into the prepared muffin tin. Bake for 20 minutes, or until a toothpick inserted in the center of a muffin comes out clean.

TIP: Shorten your prep time by using pre-shredded carrots and spiralized zucchini. Most grocery stores sell zucchini spirals in the produce section. Simply dice up enough to fill one cup and save the rest for pasta night.

PER SERVING (1 MUFFIN): Calories: 119; Fat: 1g; Protein: 3g; Carbohydrates: 25g, Fiber: 2g; Sugar: 10g; Sodium: 151mg

Mushroom and Scallion Chickpea Omelet

FAST FAV.

SERVES: 4 | **PREP TIME:** 10 MINUTES | **COOK TIME:** 15 MINUTES

This omelet base is great to have in your repertoire—it cooks quickly and works with all sorts of toppings. Make a double batch without the vegetables and store the extras in the refrigerator for up to four days to use as tasty wraps.

1 cup chickpea flour
⅓ cup nutritional yeast
½ teaspoon garlic powder
½ teaspoon freshly ground black pepper
¼ teaspoon baking powder

¼ teaspoon salt
1 cup water
1 tablespoon extra-virgin olive oil

6 white button or cremini mushrooms, stems removed and caps thinly sliced
2 scallions, both green and white parts, chopped

1. In a medium bowl, whisk together the chickpea flour, nutritional yeast, garlic powder, pepper, baking powder, and salt. Add the water and stir to form a thick but pourable batter. If your batter is thick or clumpy, add 1 tablespoon of water at a time to loosen it.

2. In a large sauté pan or skillet, heat the oil on medium-high heat. Add the mushrooms and scallions and cook for 5 to 7 minutes, or until the mushrooms are browned.

3. Pour the chickpea batter over the mushroom and scallion mix, and gently tilt the pan in a circle to spread the batter evenly over the bottom. Cook for 3 to 4 minutes, or until the underside of the omelet is lightly browned, then carefully flip the entire omelet over and cook the other side for 2 minutes.

4. Transfer to a plate, cut into 4 portions, and serve.

> **FLEX TIP:** If you like cheese in your omelet, add it to the omelet while cooking, or sprinkle on a layer of your favorite store-bought dairy-free cheese shreds.

PER SERVING: Calories: 198; Fat: 5g; Protein: 8g; Carbohydrates: 27g; Fiber: 8g; Sugar: 3g; Sodium: 185mg

Veggie and White Bean Scramble

FAST FAV. ONE-POT

SERVES: 4 | **PREP TIME:** 10 MINUTES | **COOK TIME:** 16 MINUTES

When you want a hearty, hot breakfast, this protein-rich scramble can become a family favorite. You may even find yourself making this for a quick supper.

2 tablespoons extra-virgin olive oil

1 cup yellow squash, cut into small cubes, about ½ inch

1 red bell pepper, chopped

¼ cup chopped onion

2 cloves of garlic, minced

1 (19-ounce) can cannellini beans, rinsed and drained

1 pound fresh spinach (or 1 cup frozen spinach)

1 teaspoon dried oregano

½ teaspoon dried basil

½ teaspoon salt

¼ teaspoon freshly ground black pepper

¼ teaspoon red pepper flakes (optional)

1 cup grape tomatoes, halved

1. In a large skillet, heat the olive oil over medium heat. Add the squash, bell pepper, and onion, and cook for 5 minutes, or until they start to soften. Stir occasionally.

2. Add the garlic and cook for 1 minute until fragrant.

3. Add the cannellini beans, spinach, oregano, basil, salt, pepper, and red pepper flakes (if using), and cook for 5 minutes, until the spinach is wilted.

4. Add the tomatoes and cook for 5 minutes. You want to warm up the tomatoes but not allow them to break down into a sauce.

5. Serve over toasted sourdough bread.

FLEX TIP: Cook turkey sausage (or your favorite breakfast meat) in a separate pan with a bit of olive oil and serve to those who want to eat meat. You can also substitute zucchini for the yellow squash.

PER SERVING: Calories: 225; Fat: 8g; Protein: 11g; Carbohydrates: 30g, Fiber: 12g; Sugar: 4g; Sodium: 386mg

Pear and Farro Bowl

FAST FAV. ONE-POT

SERVES: 4 | **PREP TIME:** 10 MINUTES | **COOK TIME:** 20 MINUTES

Farro is an ancient grain with a mild nutty flavor and a chewy texture like barley. It contains protein and fiber and is high in iron, calcium, and vitamins A, B, C, and E. You can dress it up savory or sweet. Here we're adding maple syrup and fruit for a slightly sweet but hearty breakfast.

1 cup pearled farro
4 cups water
Pinch salt
1 cup unsweetened almond milk

4 pears, cored and chopped, divided
1 tablespoon freshly squeezed lemon juice
2 teaspoons vanilla extract

½ teaspoon ground cinnamon
½ cup chopped walnuts
¼ cup pure maple syrup

1. Add the farro to a medium saucepan. Toast over medium heat for 2 minutes to bring out its nutty flavor. Be careful not to burn it. Add the water and a pinch of salt, and bring to a boil over medium heat.

2. Reduce the heat, cover, and let simmer for 20 minutes, or until the farro has puffed up and the liquid has absorbed.

3. Remove from the heat. Stir in the almond milk, 3 chopped pears, lemon juice, vanilla, and cinnamon.

4. Divide the mixture into 4 bowls. Sprinkle each equally with chopped walnuts and the remaining chopped pear, and drizzle with maple syrup.

TIP: You can make a batch of farro in advance and keep it in the fridge for up to 3 days.

PER SERVING: Calories: 416; Fat: 11g; Protein: 10g; Carbohydrates: 75g; Fiber: 12g; Sugar: 34g; Sodium: 62mg

Smoothie Bowls, 3 Ways

FAST FAV.   ONE-POT

SERVES: 2 | **PREP TIME:** 10 MINUTES

Here are basic instructions for how to make thick, creamy smoothie bowls, with three recipe variations. Have fun experimenting by adjusting toppings to your taste.

BERRY BLAST

2 cups frozen mixed berries   ¼ cup almond milk
1 cup frozen banana slices

TROPICAL

½ cup frozen pineapple   A large handful fresh   ¼ cup coconut water
   chunks   spinach
½ cup frozen mango chunks   1 kiwi, peeled

CREAMY DELIGHT

3 frozen bananas, sliced   1 tablespoon chia seeds
1 tablespoon raw cacao   ½ cup unsweetened almond
   powder   milk

1. Add frozen fruit and/or veggies to a blender equipped with a metal blade and blend on low until smooth but still a little chunky.

2. Add liquid ingredients and blend on low until the mixture is thick and creamy.

3. Scoop into bowls and add any desired toppings, if using. Enjoy immediately.

> **TIP:** For the Berry Blast, try topping with coconut flakes, pumpkin seeds, or banana slices; for the Tropical, try granola or coconut flakes; and for the Creamy Delight, try almond butter, sliced fresh strawberries, or granola.

BERRY BLAST PER SERVING: Calories: 185; Fat: 1g; Protein: 2g; Carbohydrates: 45g, Fiber: 7g; Sugar: 28g; Sodium: 12mg

TROPICAL PER SERVING: Calories: 76; Fat: 1g; Protein: 2g; Carbohydrates: 18g, Fiber: 3g; Sugar: 14g; Sodium: 45mg

CREAMY DELIGHT PER SERVING: Calories: 209; Fat: 3g; Protein: 4g; Carbohydrates: 47g, Fiber: 8g; Sugar: 24g; Sodium: 22mg

Polenta with Potato and Red Onion

FAST FAV.   5/FEWER ING.

SERVES: 4 | **PREP TIME:** 10 MINUTES | **COOK TIME:** 20 MINUTES

Instant polenta is a porridge made of yellow cornmeal that cooks in a few minutes. It makes a hearty base for a hot breakfast. You can dress it up sweet or savory. Here we make a flavorful breakfast with potatoes, red onion, and a hit of black pepper.

2 large russet potatoes, peeled and cut into 1-inch cubes

1 teaspoon salt, divided

3 tablespoons extra-virgin olive oil

1 red onion, thinly sliced

½ to 1 teaspoon freshly ground black pepper

1½ cups instant polenta

1. Put the potatoes in a saucepan, cover with water, add ½ teaspoon of the salt, and bring to a boil over medium-high heat. Cook for about 10 minutes, until the potatoes soften. Drain and rinse under cold running water.

2. In a large skillet, heat the olive oil over medium heat. Add the potatoes and red onion and cook, stirring occasionally, for about 10 minutes, until the potatoes start to brown and the onion softens. Sprinkle with the remaining ½ teaspoon of salt and the black pepper. I like these with a lot of black pepper, but you can adjust the pepper to your taste.

3. Meanwhile, cook the instant polenta according to the package directions in a medium saucepan over medium-high heat. It should take about 5 minutes.

4. Spoon the polenta into bowls and top with the potato and onion mixture. Add more salt and pepper to taste, if desired.

FLEX TIP: Add your favorite breakfast meat, like bacon strips or sausage links, and sprinkle with Parmesan or Romano cheese.

PER SERVING: Calories: 463; Fat: 10g; Protein: 9g; Carbohydrates: 86g, Fiber: 9g; Sugar: 2g; Sodium: 592mg

GLT Sandwich

FAST FAV.

SERVES: 4 | **PREP TIME:** 10 MINUTES

This breakfast sandwich will wake you up with a guacamole filling that has a jalapeño pepper kick. Avocados are packed with vitamins, potassium, and dietary fiber and are an excellent source of heart-healthy fats, which help your body absorb all those wonderful nutrients.

8 sourdough bread slices, toasted

¼ cup Roasted Jalapeño and Lime Guacamole (page 114)

1 large tomato, sliced

1 head of iceberg lettuce, sliced

Pinch salt

Pinch freshly ground black pepper

1. Start building the sandwiches with 4 slices of toast. Dividing equally, top each with 1 tablespoon guacamole, a slice of tomato, and a few slices of lettuce. Sprinkle with salt and pepper. Close the sandwiches with the last 4 slices of toast.

2. Cut the sandwiches diagonally and serve.

FLEX TIP: For a traditional BLT, replace the guacamole with two slices of bacon per sandwich. You can replace the sourdough with any bread of your choice.

PER SERVING: Calories: 398; Fat: 5g; Protein: 16g; Carbohydrates: 73g, Fiber: 6g; Sugar: 10g; Sodium: 609mg

Green Shakshuka

ONE-POT **QUICK PREP.**

SERVES: 2 | **PREP TIME:** 5 MINUTES | **COOK TIME:** 30 MINUTES

In this Shakshuka, we're making a version using primarily green vegetables, and we're replacing the eggs with avocado. The addition of beans makes this a hearty breakfast.

---

2 tablespoons extra-virgin olive oil

1 large leek, white and light green parts, chopped

2 cloves of garlic, minced

½ cup Vegetable Broth (page 112)

½ teaspoon salt

½ teaspoon red pepper flakes

¼ teaspoon freshly ground black pepper

1 cup frozen peas

1 (19-ounce) can cannellini beans, drained and rinsed

2 cups fresh baby spinach

Juice of half a lemon

2 tablespoons chopped flat-leaf parsley

2 avocados, halved, peeled, and pitted

4 grape tomatoes

1. In a large, deep skillet or cast-iron braising pan, warm the olive oil over medium heat. Add the leek and cook for 5 minutes, until it starts to soften. Add the garlic and cook for 1 minute until fragrant.

2. Add the vegetable broth, salt, red pepper flakes, and pepper, and cook for 5 minutes until the broth gets hot.

3. Add the frozen peas and cook for 2 minutes, until they start to thaw.

4. Add the beans, spinach, lemon juice, and parsley. Cover and cook for 5 minutes, until the spinach wilts. Remove the cover and toss everything to combine.

5. With a spoon, make 4 indentations in the mixture and add an avocado half in each one, hollow-side up. Add a grape tomato to each avocado hollow. Lower the heat to a simmer, cover, and cook for 8 to 10 minutes.

6. Sprinkle with more black pepper and serve with slices of crusty baguette.

> **FLEX TIP:** Sprinkle the top with Parmesan cheese for a salty hit of dairy. Try replacing the avocado with toasted polenta rounds.

PER SERVING: Calories: 760; Fat: 44g; Protein: 25g; Carbohydrates: 77g; Fiber: 28g; Sugar: 8g; Sodium: 138mg

Skillet Asparagus with Lemon Zest ◆ 41

CHAPTER 3

Vegetables and Sides

Red Swiss Chard with White Beans ◆ 38

Herb-Roasted Potatoes with Shallots ◆ 39

Broccoli Rabe with Red Pepper Flakes ◆ 40

Skillet Asparagus with Lemon Zest ◆ 41

Quinoa Pilaf ◆ 42

Cajun Sweet Potato Fries ◆ 43

Roasted Mediterranean Sheet Pan Vegetables ◆ 44

Easy Ratatouille ◆ 45

Baked Potato with Sherried Mushrooms ◆ 46

Mixed Veggie Slaw ◆ 47

Root Vegetable Chips ◆ 48

Red Swiss Chard with White Beans

5/FEWER ING. FAST FAV.

SERVES: 2 | **PREP TIME:** 10 MINUTES | **COOK TIME:** 15 MINUTES

Red Swiss chard has a vibrant color and a mild flavor that pairs well with protein-rich white beans. Be sure to include both the red stems and tender green leaves in this energy-boosting dish.

1 (15-ounce) can cannellini beans, undrained

1 tablespoon extra-virgin olive oil

1 bunch red Swiss chard, stems and leaves cut into 1-inch pieces and kept separate

1 small tomato, chopped

1 clove of garlic, minced

Pinch salt

Pinch freshly ground black pepper

1. Pour the cannellini beans and their liquid into a small saucepan. Bring to a boil over medium heat, then reduce to a simmer.

2. Meanwhile, in a skillet, heat the olive oil over medium heat. Add a splash of water and the chard stems, cover, and cook until they start to soften, about 5 minutes.

3. Add the tomato and garlic to the chard stems and cook for 1 minute, uncovered, then add the chard leaves, salt, and pepper. Cook until the leaves wilt, about 3 minutes more.

4. Drain the beans and add them to the chard mixture. Cook for 2 minutes, until just blended.

FLEX TIP: Add chopped, cooked turkey bacon or leftover pork to the skillet with the chard leaves for a Southern-style dish.

PER SERVING: Calories: 303; Fat: 8g; Protein: 16g; Carbohydrates: 44g; Fiber: 13g; Sugar: 3g; Sodium: 318mg

Herb-Roasted Potatoes with Shallots

FAST FAV.

SERVES: 4 | **PREP TIME:** 10 MINUTES | **COOK TIME:** 15 MINUTES

White potatoes have their place in a Mediterranean diet; they are a healthy and all-natural source of carbohydrates, vitamins, and minerals. Roasted shallots amp up the flavor of this simple dish.

¼ cup extra-virgin olive oil, plus more for brushing

2 large russet potatoes, peeled and cut into 1-inch cubes

1 teaspoon salt

½ teaspoon garlic powder

½ teaspoon smoked paprika

½ teaspoon dried oregano

¼ teaspoon dried rosemary

¼ teaspoon dried thyme

¼ teaspoon red pepper flakes (optional)

2 or 3 shallots, cut into large chunks

1. Preheat the oven to 425°F. Line a rimmed baking sheet with aluminum foil and brush with olive oil.

2. In a large bowl, toss the potatoes with olive oil, salt, garlic powder, paprika, oregano, rosemary, thyme, and red pepper flakes (if using).

3. Pour the potatoes onto the baking sheet and spread them out in a single layer. Scatter the shallots around the potatoes.

4. Bake for 15 to 20 minutes until everything looks golden brown with crispy edges.

FLEX TIP: A generous sprinkle of Parmesan cheese added 10 minutes before the potatoes are done creates a wonderful salty, rich accent.

PER SERVING: Calories: 271; Fat: 14g; Protein: 4g; Carbohydrates: 35g, Fiber: 3g; Sugar: 2g; Sodium: 592mg

Broccoli Rabe with Red Pepper Flakes

5/FEWER ING. **FAST FAV.** **QUICK PREP.**

SERVES: 2 | **PREP TIME:** 5 MINUTES | **COOK TIME:** 10 MINUTES

Broccoli rabe, also known as rapini, is a cruciferous vegetable that is like broccoli in flavor. Red pepper flakes complement its mild bitterness by adding a subtle amount of heat. This classic side dish hails from southern Italy.

1 pound broccoli rabe, thick stems trimmed

2 tablespoons extra-virgin olive oil

1 clove of garlic, minced

Salt

Freshly ground black pepper

¼ teaspoon red pepper flakes

1. Bring a large pot of water to a boil over high heat. Add the broccoli rabe and cook for 3 minutes. Drain. When cool enough to handle, cut the broccoli rabe into bite-size pieces.

2. In a large skillet, heat the olive oil over medium heat. Add the broccoli rabe and garlic, season with salt and black pepper, and cook for 4 to 5 minutes, until tender.

3. Sprinkle the red pepper flakes over the top of the dish just before serving.

FLEX TIP: Turn this into a complete meal by adding 2 cups chopped, cooked chicken and 4 cups cooked whole-grain penne or rotini to the skillet and tossing until heated through.

PER SERVING: Calories: 171; Fat: 15g; Protein: 7g; Carbohydrates: 7g; Fiber: 6g; Sugar: 1g; Sodium: 153mg

Skillet Asparagus with Lemon Zest

5/FEWER ING. | **FAST FAV.** | **ONE-POT**

SERVES: 4 | **PREP TIME:** 10 MINUTES | **COOK TIME:** 10 MINUTES

This simple preparation brings out the inherent deliciousness of asparagus. Tart citrus perks up the taste buds without overpowering the flavor of this slender vegetable. When a recipe calls for lemon zest, use organic lemons whenever possible, or scrub regular lemons with a soft-bristled brush before zesting. Conventionally grown lemons are coated with a layer of wax to protect them during shipping, and you do not want to add that wax to this lovely dish.

¼ cup extra-virgin olive oil

2 pounds asparagus, woody ends trimmed

3 to 4 cloves of garlic, minced

Zest of 1 medium lemon

Pinch salt, plus more as needed

Pinch freshly ground black pepper, plus more as needed

Red pepper flakes (optional)

1. In a large skillet, heat the olive oil over medium-high heat. Add the asparagus and stir to coat with the oil. Sauté for 3 minutes, then add the garlic, lemon zest, salt, and black pepper and sauté for 5 to 7 minutes, until the asparagus is tender-crisp.

2. Taste and adjust the seasonings, then serve.

FLEX TIP: This asparagus is great served alongside your favorite lamb or fish dish.

PER SERVING: Calories: 171; Fat: 14g; Protein: 5g; Carbohydrates: 10g, Fiber: 6g; Sugar: 5g; Sodium: 44mg

Quinoa Pilaf

FAST FAV.	ONE-POT

SERVES: 4 | **PREP TIME:** 10 MINUTES | **COOK TIME:** 20 MINUTES

To make an everyday grain special, simply add vegetables. When you're bulk cooking on the weekend and thinking, "No more brown rice," add some veggies and see how that changes your opinion. In this case, by adding onion and carrots to quinoa, this "side" becomes a hearty entrée.

½ cup chopped red onion
1 cup diced carrots
½ teaspoon dried parsley
½ teaspoon dried thyme

1 cup dry quinoa, rinsed and drained
1½ cups Vegetable Broth (page 112)

¼ cup chopped walnuts
Chopped fresh parsley or thyme, for garnish

1. In a large saucepan, dry sauté the onion and carrots over medium-high heat, stirring frequently to prevent sticking, until the onion is tender, 3 to 5 minutes. Add the parsley, thyme, quinoa, and broth and bring to a boil.

2. Lower the heat to medium-low, cover, and cook for 15 minutes. Remove the pan from the heat and let sit for 5 minutes.

3. Fluff the quinoa with a fork, add the walnuts, and gently mix until combined.

4. Spoon into bowls and serve garnished with fresh parsley.

> **TIP:** If you like to cook plain grains in bulk—think rice, farro, and millet—you can transform them by sautéing onion and carrot in a skillet as directed in this recipe adding 1 or 2 cups cooked grains (no vegetable broth), and stir-frying until hot.

PER SERVING (1½ CUPS): Calories: 230; Fat: 7g; Protein: 8g; Carbohydrates: 34g, Fiber: 5g; Sugar: 3g; Sodium: 37mg

Cajun Sweet Potato Fries

QUICK PREP.

SERVES: 4 | **PREP TIME:** 5 MINUTES | **COOK TIME:** 30 MINUTES

Cajun spices, with their mild heat, perfectly complement the sweetness of sweet potatoes. These "fries" are cooked in the oven for a healthier side dish. If you don't want to make your own Cajun blend, you can also find it premade at the supermarket—you'll need 2 tablespoons for this recipe.

---

3 medium-size sweet potatoes

2 tablespoons extra-virgin olive oil

2 teaspoons salt

1½ teaspoons paprika

1 teaspoon freshly ground black pepper

1 teaspoon dried oregano

½ teaspoon garlic powder

½ teaspoon onion powder

½ teaspoon cayenne pepper

3 or 4 fresh thyme sprigs

1. Preheat the oven to 425°F. Prepare a baking sheet with nonstick cooking spray.

2. Wash the sweet potatoes in cold water and pat dry. Cut in half lengthwise, then cut each half lengthwise into four slices to form similar-sized wedges.

3. In a large mixing bowl, toss the potatoes, olive oil, salt, paprika, pepper, oregano, garlic powder, onion powder, and cayenne.

4. Arrange the thyme sprigs on the baking sheet. Turn out the potato blend on top in a single layer, cut-sides down. I like to put the thyme underneath the potatoes, so it doesn't burn.

5. Bake for 15 minutes, turn the potatoes over and cook for another 15 minutes, or until cooked through. Discard the thyme sprigs.

6. Sprinkle with more salt before serving, if desired.

> **TIP:** The Cajun spice blend also works well as a shrimp, chicken, or fish seasoning while cooking. You can even sprinkle this blend on popcorn instead of butter.

PER SERVING: Calories: 150; Fat: 7g; Protein: 2g; Carbohydrates: 21g; Fiber: 4g; Sugar: 4g; Sodium: 1218mg

Roasted Mediterranean Sheet Pan Vegetables

ONE-POT

SERVES: 4 | **PREP TIME**: 15 MINUTES | **COOK TIME**: 30 MINUTES

Roasted vegetables are an excellent side dish or perfect on their own, served over rice, or tossed with pasta. They also make a tasty sandwich filler. Make a batch of these vegetables and use them throughout the week.

Nonstick cooking spray

1 zucchini, cut into long ribbons with a peeler

1 yellow squash, cut into long ribbons with a peeler

1 red bell pepper, seeded and cut into 1-inch chunks

12 grape tomatoes

3 shallots, peeled and quartered

5 cloves of garlic, ends trimmed off and unpeeled

3 tablespoons extra-virgin olive oil

1 teaspoon salt

½ teaspoon freshly ground black pepper

3 rosemary sprigs

1. Preheat the oven to 400°F. Line a baking sheet with foil and nonstick cooking spray.

2. In a large bowl, combine zucchini, squash, bell pepper, tomatoes, shallots, and garlic. Add the olive oil, salt, and pepper, and toss to coat. Arrange evenly over the baking sheet. It's all right if they overlap. Place rosemary sprigs on top.

3. Roast for 15 minutes, toss, and then roast for another 10 to 15 minutes until the vegetables are tender.

4. Remove the cloves of garlic from their skins. They should pop right out at this point. Discard the rosemary before serving.

TIP: Refrigerate the leftovers in an airtight container for up to 3 days.

PER SERVING: Calories: 136; Fat: 11g; Protein: 2g; Carbohydrates: 9g; Fiber: 3g; Sugar: 6g; Sodium: 595mg

Easy Ratatouille

ONE-POT

SERVES: 4 | **PREP TIME**: 15 MINUTES | **COOK TIME**: 36 MINUTES

Make a large pot of this fragrant vegetable dish for a French-inspired dinner, or eat it as a side dish or smaller lunch portion throughout the week. You can also safely freeze it for up to 3 months if you want to save some for a later date.

¼ cup extra-virgin olive oil

2 onions, chopped

4 cloves of garlic minced

2 eggplant, peeled, seeds removed, cut into 1-inch cubes

4 zucchini, cut into 1-inch cubes

3 red bell peppers, seeded and cut into 1-inch cubes

2 teaspoons salt

1 teaspoon freshly ground black pepper

1 (28-ounce) can diced tomatoes

1 tablespoon herbes de Provence

To make your own herbes de Provence:

1 teaspoon dried basil

1 teaspoon dried thyme

½ teaspoon dried marjoram

½ teaspoon fennel

½ teaspoon dried lavender flowers

1. In a Dutch oven or a large pot with a tight-fitting lid, heat oil over medium heat. Add the onions and cook for 5 minutes until they start to soften. Add the garlic and cook for 1 minute, until fragrant.

2. Add the eggplant, zucchini, bell pepper, salt, black pepper, and ¾ cup water. Stir well, cover, and bring to a boil. Reduce the heat, and simmer for 10 minutes until the vegetables start to soften.

3. Stir in the tomatoes and herbes de Provence. Reduce the heat to low. Leave the lid partially ajar, and simmer for 20 minutes, until vegetables are tender, stirring frequently.

4. Serve with sliced crusty French baguette.

FLEX TIP: Sprinkle generously with Parmesan or Romano cheese. Serve with pan-fried or grilled andouille sausage.

PER SERVING: Calories: 307; Fat: 16g; Protein: 9g; Carbohydrates: 41g, Fiber: 15g; Sugar: 25g; Sodium: 1,419mg

Baked Potato with Sherried Mushrooms

FAST FAV. | QUICK PREP.

SERVES: 4 | **PREP TIME:** 5 MINUTES | **COOK TIME:** 17 MINUTES

---

4 large russet potatoes

½ teaspoon salt, divided

3 tablespoons extra-virgin olive oil

12 ounces white mushrooms, sliced

¼ teaspoon freshly ground black pepper

2 cloves of garlic, thinly sliced

1 tablespoon vegan butter or margarine

2 teaspoons fresh thyme leaves

¼ cup cream sherry

1. Wash the potatoes well, and while still wet, sprinkle all around with ¼ teaspoon of salt. Pierce each potato skin 3 to 4 times with a fork.

2. Place the potatoes on a microwavable plate, cook on full power for 5 minutes, turn over, and cook for another 5 minutes. Check for doneness. Depending on your microwave and the size of the potatoes, you may need an additional 2 minutes.

3. In the meantime, heat the oil in a large skillet over medium heat. Cook the mushrooms for 5 minutes without stirring.

4. Toss the mushrooms and add the remaining ¼ teaspoon of salt and black pepper. Cook for another 5 minutes until the mushrooms are browned.

5. Add the garlic, margarine, and thyme, and cook for 2 minutes until fragrant.

6. Add the sherry, and cook until evaporated, about 5 minutes.

7. Remove the potatoes from the oven. Split them down the middle and equally divide the mushroom mixture onto each potato. Serve.

TIP: No microwave? Preheat to 450°F. Prep the potatoes as in step 1. Place directly on the oven rack and roast for 45 minutes, or until soft all the way through.

PER SERVING: Calories: 427; Fat: 14g; Protein: 11g; Carbohydrates: 70g; Fiber: 6g; Sugar: 4g; Sodium: 315mg

Mixed Veggie Slaw

$$\boxed{\text{FAST FAV.}}$$

SERVES: 4 TO 6 | **PREP TIME:** 15 MINUTES

A cool slaw makes a great side dish or topping for sandwiches. You may even find you want to eat this tasty slaw as a salad on its own. The beauty of this recipe is that you can vary the ingredients to suit your tastes and moods by varying the vegetables and fruits you use.

¼ cup coconut yogurt

2 teaspoons freshly squeezed lime juice

2 teaspoons pure maple syrup

1 teaspoon Dijon mustard

¼ teaspoon salt

4 cups shredded vegetables and/or fruit (cabbage, carrots, cucumbers, or apples)

2 tablespoons of chopped fresh herbs (green onion, dill, parsley, or cilantro)

1. In a large bowl, whisk the yogurt, lime juice, maple syrup, mustard, and salt.

2. Add the veggies and herbs to the dressing, toss, and serve.

FLEX TIP: You can use nonfat Greek yogurt instead of coconut yogurt for lower sugar content. Replace the maple syrup with honey.

PER SERVING: Calories: 53; Fat: 0g; Protein: 2g; Carbohydrates: 12g, Fiber: 2g; Sugar: 6g; Sodium: 189mg

Root Vegetable Chips

FAST FAV.   5/FEWER ING.

SERVES: 4 | **PREP TIME:** 10 MINUTES | **COOK TIME:** 20 MINUTES

Baked vegetable chips are a fun snack to make and a healthier option when you are craving deep-fried potato chips. The colors are enticing, and you can play around with the seasonings.

4 root vegetables, such as sweet potatoes, purple potatoes, beets, turnips, rutabagas, or parsnips

1 tablespoon extra-virgin olive oil

1 teaspoon salt

1 teaspoon smoked paprika

1. Preheat the oven to 400°F. Line a baking sheet with parchment paper.

2. Thinly slice the vegetables using a vegetable peeler, a mandoline, or the slicing slide of a box grater. Alternatively, you could finely slice the vegetables by hand. You want them as thin as possible.

3. Pat the vegetables dry with a paper towel. In a large bowl, toss the vegetables with oil, salt, and paprika. Mix with your hands until evenly coated.

4. Arrange them on the baking sheet without overlapping the vegetables. Bake for 17 to 20 minutes until crispy. Keep an eye on them as some vegetables may cook more quickly than others, and the cooking time varies depending on how thick or thin you slice the vegetables.

5. Allow the chips to cool and serve.

> **TIP:** Have fun experimenting with seasoning. Here are some possible combinations: 1 teaspoon salt with ¼ teaspoon cayenne, 1 teaspoon salt with ½ teaspoon rosemary and ½ teaspoon thyme, 1 teaspoon salt with 1 teaspoon garlic powder, or 1 teaspoon salt with 1 teaspoon mixed Italian dry herbs.

PER SERVING: Calories: 131; Fat: 3g; Protein: 3g; Carbohydrates: 23g; Fiber: 4g; Sugar: 4g; Sodium: 620mg

Panzanella Salad ◆ 55

CHAPTER 4

Salads and Handhelds

Massaged Kale Salad ◆ 52

Chopped Avocado Chickpea Salad with Olives ◆ 53

Mediterranean Potato Salad ◆ 54

Panzanella Salad ◆ 55

Ancient Grains Salad ◆ 56

Pizza Pockets ◆ 57

Salad with Peach Carpaccio ◆ 58

Nouveau Greek Salad ◆ 59

Pearl Couscous Salad ◆ 60

Roasted Fennel, Lentil, and Apple Salad ◆ 61

Roasted Vegetable Flatbread ◆ 62

Family-Style Taco Bar ◆ 63

Massaged Kale Salad

5/FEWER ING. **FAST FAV.** **ONE-POT**

SERVES: 4 | **PREP TIME:** 10 MINUTES

Did you know that to enjoy kale raw, all you need to do is give it a gentle massage with a little fat and acid to break it down and make it easier to eat and digest? When you do, the volume reduces (sometimes by nearly half) and the color becomes a deep green. The addition of hemp seeds creates a texture like Parmesan, and they cling to the tahini-coated kale leaves. Serve the salad as is or power it up with baked tofu or roasted chickpeas.

2 bunches kale, leaves stemmed and torn into bite-size pieces

¼ cup tahini

¼ cup freshly squeezed lemon juice

2 cloves of garlic, minced

¼ cup hemp seeds

1 teaspoon salt

1. Place the kale in a large bowl. Add the tahini, lemon juice, and garlic. With clean or gloved hands, massage the kale until it brightens and glistens and the leaves are coated, about 3 minutes.

2. Sprinkle the hemp seeds and salt over the salad and toss gently, then serve.

> **TIP:** Peanut, almond, and sunflower seed butters are all fantastic substitutes for the tahini. Lime or orange juice can be used instead of lemon juice.

PER SERVING (2 CUPS): Calories: 162; Fat: 13g; Protein: 6g; Carbohydrates: 9g; Fiber: 3g; Sugar: 1g; Sodium: 31mg

Chopped Avocado Chickpea Salad with Olives

FAST FAV.

SERVES: 6 | **PREP TIME:** 15 MINUTES

The chickpeas give this salad added protein and fiber, and the avocado adds a creaminess that pairs well with the snappy bite from the onion and parsley. Serve this salad with falafel and hummus for a Middle Eastern–style feast.

FOR THE DRESSING

¼ cup grapeseed or extra-virgin olive oil

3 tablespoons red wine or apple cider vinegar

Juice of ½ lemon

¼ teaspoon salt

¼ teaspoon freshly ground black pepper

FOR THE SALAD

1 (15-ounce) can chickpeas, drained and rinsed

2 medium seedless cucumbers, diced

1 pint grape tomatoes, halved

1 yellow bell pepper, seeded and diced

1 avocado, peeled, pitted, and diced

1 cup sliced Kalamata or black olives

½ cup diced red onion

½ cup chopped fresh flat-leaf parsley

TO MAKE THE DRESSING:

1. In a jar with a tight-fitting lid, combine the oil, vinegar, lemon juice, salt, and pepper. Cover tightly and shake to combine.

TO MAKE THE SALAD

2. In a large bowl, combine the chickpeas, cucumbers, tomatoes, bell pepper, avocado, olives, red onion, and parsley. Add the dressing, toss to combine, and serve.

TIP: This salad is delicious tucked into pita bread or wrapped in a tortilla for a filling grab-and-go sandwich.

PER SERVING: Calories: 247; Fat: 17g; Protein: 6g; Carbohydrates: 22g, Fiber: 7g; Sugar: 5g; Sodium: 327mg

Mediterranean Potato Salad

FAST FAV.

SERVES: 6 | **PREP TIME:** 15 MINUTES | **COOK TIME:** 15 MINUTES

This potato salad is very refreshing. The lemon vinaigrette is lighter than traditional mayonnaise-based potato salad dressings. You can make this salad a day before serving, and it will last a week in the refrigerator.

4 russet potatoes

1 red bell pepper, seeded and finely diced

1 red onion, finely chopped

2 cups chopped fresh parsley

½ cup capers, drained

¼ cup extra-virgin olive oil

¼ cup freshly squeezed lemon juice

Grated zest of 1 lemon

1 teaspoon dried thyme

⅛ teaspoon salt

1. Place the potatoes in a medium saucepan, cover with cold water, and bring to a boil over medium-high heat. Cook for about 15 minutes, until the potatoes are soft but not over-cooked. You want to be able to pierce them with a fork but have them stay whole. Drain and let cool.

2. Peel the potatoes and cut them into ½-inch cubes. Place the potatoes in a medium bowl.

3. Add the red bell pepper, red onion, parsley, and capers to the bowl and set aside.

4. In a small bowl, whisk the olive oil, lemon juice, lemon zest, thyme, and salt until well combined. Drizzle the dressing over the potato salad and toss until well coated. Serve chilled or at room temperature.

FLEX TIP: Although not the mayo-based version, this salad is enhanced by the addition of sliced hard-boiled eggs. Add them at the end on top of the salad rather than stirring them in.

PER SERVING: Calories: 211; Fat: 9g; Protein: 4g; Carbohydrates: 31g, Fiber: 4g; Sugar: 3g; Sodium: 312mg

Panzanella Salad

> FAST FAV.

SERVES: 6 | **PREP TIME:** 20 MINUTES | **COOK TIME:** 5 MINUTES

The word "panzanella" comes from two Italian words: *pane,* meaning "bread," and *zanella,* meaning "soup bowl." For a fun presentation, make individual panzanella bowls by placing a slice of olive bread in a salad bowl, topping it with chopped vegetables, and drizzling the dressing all over.

1 small loaf French bread, cut into 1-inch cubes (about 6 cups)

¼ cup extra-virgin olive oil, divided

3 large tomatoes

2 Persian cucumbers, cut into ½-inch-thick rounds

1 small red onion, thinly sliced

1 cup chopped fresh basil

1 clove of garlic, mashed to a paste

¼ cup red wine vinegar

⅛ teaspoon salt

1. Preheat the oven to 350°F.

2. In a large bowl, toss the bread cubes with 2 tablespoons of olive oil until coated. Spread the cubes in a single layer on a baking sheet. Bake for 5 minutes or until the bread is lightly toasted. Divide the toasted cubes evenly among serving bowls.

3. Dice the tomatoes into a colander set over a bowl to collect the juices. Transfer the tomatoes to a medium bowl and set the bowl containing the juice aside.

4. Add the cucumbers, red onion, basil, and garlic to the tomatoes.

5. Add the remaining 2 tablespoons of olive oil, the vinegar, and salt to the bowl containing the tomato juice and whisk until well combined. Drizzle the dressing over the vegetables and toss well to mix.

6. Divide the vegetables and dressing among the bowls with the bread and serve.

FLEX TIP: Add 4 slices of cooked and crumbled bacon to the salad during step 4 for a BLT-inspired take on panzanella.

PER SERVING: Calories: 348; Fat: 18g; Protein: 10g; Carbohydrates: 41g; Fiber: 3g; Sugar: 7g; Sodium: 293mg

Ancient Grains Salad

ONE-POT

SERVES: 6 | **PREP TIME:** 20 MINUTES | **COOK TIME:** 55 MINUTES

Ancient grains are making their way back into kitchens because of their nutritional benefits and flavor. Farro is nutty tasting and cooks to a chewy texture. Rye berries are nutrient dense and have a high level of magnesium, which helps stabilize the body's glucose absorption. Both grains offer a high amount of soluble fiber, which aids digestion and blood sugar levels.

¼ cup farro

¼ cup raw rye berries

2 ripe pears, cored and coarsely chopped

2 celery ribs, coarsely chopped

1 green apple, cored and coarsely chopped

½ cup chopped fresh parsley

¼ cup golden raisins

3 tablespoons freshly squeezed lemon juice

¼ teaspoon ground cumin

Pinch cayenne pepper

1. In an 8-quart pot, combine the farro, rye berries, and enough water to cover by 3 inches. Bring to a boil over high heat. Reduce the heat to medium-low, cover the pot, and cook for 45 to 50 minutes, or until the grains are firm and chewy but not hard. Drain and set aside to cool.

2. In a large bowl, gently stir together the cooled grains, pears, celery, apple, parsley, raisins, lemon juice, cumin, and cayenne pepper. Serve immediately or refrigerate in an airtight container for up to 1 week.

TIP: Many grains are suitable for this recipe. The goal is to use whole grains, like farro, rye, wheat berries, or kamut, to get the most fiber and mineral benefits from the full grain. You can also cook the grains ahead to make a weekday meal even easier.

PER SERVING: Calories: 127; Fat: 1g; Protein: 3g; Carbohydrates: 31g, Fiber: 5g; Sugar: 14g; Sodium: 16mg

Pizza Pockets

FAST FAV.

SERVES: 4 | **PREP TIME:** 10 MINUTES | **COOK TIME:** 20 MINUTES

Here is a vegan alternative to a stromboli or calzone. Don't worry if it sounds complicated—this recipe uses store-bought pizza dough, so it is a snap to make and bakes quickly in the time it takes to make a side salad. To make the meal even easier, use your favorite store-bought sauce.

All-purpose flour, for rolling
1 (1-pound) ball store-bought pizza dough
1 cup Basic Tomato Basil Sauce (page 115)

½ cup shredded mozzarella-style vegan cheese
½ cup sliced mushrooms
½ cup sliced green bell pepper

½ cup sliced red onion
2 tablespoons extra-virgin olive oil
1 tablespoon Italian seasoning

1. Preheat the oven to 425°F. Line a rimmed baking sheet with parchment paper and set aside.

2. On a floured surface, roll out the dough into a rectangle about ½-inch thick. Cut into 8 rectangles. On one half of each rectangle, add about 1 tablespoon of sauce and top with 1 tablespoon each of cheese, mushrooms, green peppers, and onion. Fold, sealing all edges by pressing them down with a fork, and transfer the pockets to the baking sheet.

3. In a small bowl, mix the oil and Italian seasoning. Gently brush the tops of each pizza pocket with the seasoned oil.

4. Bake for 20 minutes, until the dough looks crisp and golden. Serve immediately.

FLEX TIP: Try adding pepperoni slices or crumbled cooked sausage for a meat variation.

PER SERVING: Calories: 415; Fat: 14g; Protein: 12g; Carbohydrates: 62g; Fiber: 4g; Sugar: 12g; Sodium: 757mg

Salad with Peach Carpaccio

(FAST FAV.)

SERVES: 4 | **PREP TIME:** 15 MINUTES

This recipe is inspired by a salad I had in an Italian restaurant in Beverly Hills, California. The base layer is made of thinly sliced peaches. The dressing has a mild kick from adding red pepper flakes to the vinaigrette.

FOR THE SALAD

2 peaches, thinly sliced

4 cups mixed lettuces (arugula, red and green leaf, baby spinach)

1 orange bell pepper, seeded and sliced

1 cucumber, sliced

2 scallions, chopped

4 radishes, sliced

FOR THE DRESSING

⅓ cup extra-virgin olive oil

¼ cup white wine vinegar

½ teaspoon dried oregano

½ teaspoon salt

¼ teaspoon freshly ground black pepper

¼ teaspoon red pepper flakes

1. Arrange the peach slices in a circular pattern on a serving plate.

2. In a large bowl, toss the lettuce, bell pepper, cucumber, scallion, and radish.

3. In a small bowl, whisk the oil, vinegar, oregano, salt, pepper, and red pepper flakes until combined. Add the dressing to the bowl with the salad ingredients and toss to combine.

4. Arrange the salad on top of the peaches. Serve.

> **FLEX TIP:** This salad goes very well with dollops of goat cheese. For the fruits and vegetables, you can get very thin slices with a mandoline or use the slicing slide of a box grater.

PER SERVING: Calories: 222; Fat: 18g; Protein: 2g; Carbohydrates: 14g, Fiber: 3g; Sugar: 8g; Sodium: 303mg

Nouveau Greek Salad

FAST FAV.

SERVES: 2 | **PREP TIME:** 15 MINUTES

This nouveau Greek salad has added spinach, and the sweet peppers are replaced with hot ones. I also swapped out the chunks of feta cheese for creamy butter beans. Serve with fresh rye bread for a little more substance to the meal.

FOR THE SALAD

4 cups fresh baby spinach leaves

1 cucumber, peeled, seeded, and chopped

1 cup grape tomatoes, halved

¼ cup pitted Kalamata olives, halved

½ small red onion, thinly sliced

4 to 6 pickled peperoncini, sliced

1 (15-ounce) can of butter beans, drained and rinsed

FOR THE DRESSING

½ cup extra-virgin olive oil

2 tablespoons red wine vinegar

2 tablespoons freshly squeezed lemon juice

1 clove of garlic, minced

1 teaspoon dried oregano

½ teaspoon dried mint

½ teaspoon salt

¼ teaspoon freshly ground black pepper

1. Combine the spinach, cucumber, tomatoes, olives, red onion, peperoncini, and beans in a large mixing bowl.

2. Prepare the dressing by placing the oil, vinegar, lemon juice, garlic, oregano, mint, salt, and pepper in a glass jar with a lid. Shake well to combine. Pour the dressing over the salad and toss to combine. Serve.

FLEX TIP: To make the dressing creamier add 1 ounce crumbled feta cheese and 3 tablespoons plain Greek yogurt. You can also serve the salad topped with crumbles of feta cheese.

PER SERVING: Calories: 737; Fat: 57g; Protein: 15g; Carbohydrates: 46g; Fiber: 16g; Sugar: 5g; Sodium: 763mg

Pearl Couscous Salad

FAST FAV.

SERVES: 4 | **PREP TIME:** 15 MINUTES | **COOK TIME:** 8 MINUTES

Couscous is often thought to be a grain because of its appearance, but it is a form of pasta. It comes in tiny particles or in tiny pearls. The pearl shape—also known as Israeli couscous—works well in salads. It absorbs the flavors of the dressing, making a wonderful lunch or side dish.

FOR THE SALAD

1 pound pearl couscous

½ small red onion, thinly sliced

1 (15-ounce) can chickpeas, drained and rinsed

1 cup grape tomatoes, halved

½ cup toasted pine nuts (or your favorite nut)

½ cup finely chopped flat-leaf parsley

1 tablespoon capers

FOR THE DRESSING

¼ cup extra-virgin olive oil

2 tablespoons freshly squeezed lemon juice

1 teaspoon lemon zest

½ teaspoon ground cumin

½ teaspoon salt

¼ teaspoon freshly ground black pepper

Pinch ground cinnamon

1. Bring a large pot of salted water to boil and cook couscous according to package instructions for al dente, about 7 to 8 minutes. Drain and rinse under cold water.

2. In a large bowl, combine the couscous, onion, chickpeas, tomatoes, pine nuts, parsley, and capers.

3. In a small bowl, whisk together the olive oil, lemon juice, lemon zest, cumin, salt, pepper, and cinnamon.

4. Pour dressing over the couscous mixture and toss well to combine. Serve at room temperature.

TIP: You could use whole wheat couscous for an added boost of whole grains.

PER SERVING: Calories: 776; Fat: 28g; Protein: 23g; Carbohydrates: 110g, Fiber: 12g; Sugar: 5g; Sodium: 364mg

Roasted Fennel, Lentil, and Apple Salad

5/FEWER ING.   FAST FAV.

SERVES: 4 | **PREP TIME:** 10 MINUTES | **COOK TIME:** 20 MINUTES

Fennel is wonderful in salad raw or cooked. Raw fennel has a bright anise flavor while cooked fennel has a creamy sweetness. Combined with the earthiness of the lentils and the crisp apple, this salad makes a unique treat for lunch or dinner.

FOR THE SALAD

1 cup French green lentils, rinsed

Pinch salt

2 fennel bulbs, core removed, thinly sliced

2 tablespoons extra-virgin olive oil

1 apple, peeled, cored, and diced

FOR THE VINAIGRETTE

¼ cup extra-virgin olive oil

Juice of half a lemon

½ teaspoon salt

¼ teaspoon freshly ground black pepper

1 teaspoon chopped fresh mint

1. Preheat oven to 350°F. Line a baking sheet with parchment paper.

2. In a medium saucepan, place lentils with enough water to cover them. Add a pinch of salt. Cover, bring to a boil, and reduce heat and simmer for 20 minutes, or until tender. Drain, and set aside to cool.

3. Place the fennel on the baking sheet and toss with olive oil to evenly coat. Spread the fennel out in a single layer and bake for 15 minutes, or until soft.

4. Whisk together the olive oil, lemon juice, salt, pepper, and mint in a small bowl.

5. In a large bowl, combine the lentils, fennel, and vinaigrette. Toss to combine and serve topped with chopped apple.

FLEX TIP: For a seafood option, top with baked cod, or even grilled shrimp.

PER SERVING: Calories: 409; Fat: 21g; Protein: 13g; Carbohydrates: 46g; Fiber: 10g; Sugar: 10g; Sodium: 394mg

Roasted Vegetable Flatbread

FAST FAV. QUICK PREP.

SERVES: 4 | **PREP TIME:** 5 MINUTES | **COOK TIME:** 10 MINUTES

Pita bread is a vegan flatbread used in Greek and Middle Eastern cuisine. One pita round per person is the ideal serving size for a satisfying lunch. The rest of this dish uses recipes from other chapters, but you can use store-bought pesto and leftovers if that is easier. This makes a fun lunch or snack and is a tasty accompaniment to soup.

4 (6-inch) pita breads
4 teaspoons Plant Pesto (page 113)

2 cups Roasted Mediterranean Sheet Pan Vegetables (page 44)

Extra-virgin olive oil, for drizzling

1. Preheat the oven to 350°F. Line a baking sheet with parchment or foil.

2. Place the pitas on the baking sheet and brush 1 teaspoon of pesto on each round. Top each with ½ cup of the vegetable mix.

3. Bake for 5 to 10 minutes to warm everything up. You don't need to toast it.

4. Drizzle with olive oil before serving.

FLEX TIP: Sprinkle on feta or Parmesan cheese. Add a scrambled egg to make a quick breakfast sandwich.

PER SERVING: Calories: 262; Fat: 10g; Protein: 7g; Carbohydrates: 39g, Fiber: 3g; Sugar: 4g; Sodium: 594mg

Family-Style Taco Bar

SERVES: 4 TO 6 | **PREP TIME:** 20 MINUTES | **COOK TIME:** 15 MINUTES

This is a fun meal for a weekend night, or even a festive spread for game day. Select small dishes and ingredients and allow your diners to pick and choose what to add to their soft or hard-shell tacos. The leftovers are ideal for a fabulous bowl the next day.

¼ cup extra-virgin olive oil

2 large onions, sliced

2 bell peppers (any color), seeded and sliced

Pinch salt

2 tomatoes, chopped

½ small onion, chopped

2 cloves of garlic, minced

1 teaspoon dried oregano

1 teaspoon salt

¼ teaspoon freshly ground black pepper

2 tablespoons extra-virgin olive oil

Vegan tortillas (selection of soft and hard); most tortillas on the market are now vegan

1 (15-ounce) can black beans, heated through with their juices

1 (15-ounce) can pinto beans, heated through with their juices

½ cup sliced pickled jalapeño peppers

1 recipe Roasted Jalapeño and Lime Guacamole (page 114)

A selection of vegetables (shredded cabbage, shredded lettuce, chopped tomatoes, diced red onion, chopped scallions, chopped fresh cilantro)

1. Heat the olive oil in a large skillet over medium-high heat, add the onion, peppers, and a pinch of salt, and sauté for 10 to 15 minutes, until soft. Transfer the mixture to a small bowl to serve as a taco ingredient.

2. In a medium bowl, combine the tomatoes, onion, garlic, oregano, salt, pepper, and olive oil, and toss to combine.

3. Arrange all the ingredients on the table and allow your guests to build their own tacos.

FLEX TIP: Add a bowl of shredded cheese such as cheddar or Monterey Jack. Add a bowl of sour cream. Sauté some shrimp or shredded chicken in a little olive oil with salt and pepper.

PER SERVING: Calories: 590; Fat: 30g; Protein: 17g; Carbohydrates: 68g, Fiber: 19g; Sugar: 11g; Sodium: 849mg

Coconut Curry Ramen ◆ 70

CHAPTER 5

Soups and Stews

Classic Vegetable Soup ◆ 66

Spicy Corn Chowder ◆ 67

Root Vegetable Soup ◆ 68

Asparagus and Leek Soup ◆ 69

Coconut Curry Ramen ◆ 70

Minestrone with Beans ◆ 71

Vegetable and Lentil Stew ◆ 72

Pea and Zucchini Soup ◆ 73

Smoky Eggplant and Yellow Squash Soup ◆ 74

Spinach Orzo Soup ◆ 75

Potato Leek Soup ◆ 76

Easy Gazpacho ◆ 78

Classic Vegetable Soup

FAST FAV.   **ONE-POT**

SERVES: 4 TO 6 | **PREP TIME:** 10 MINUTES | **COOK TIME:** 20 MINUTES

Simplicity is underrated. Start with vegetables and spices you always have on hand and add a bit of miso paste for its umami flavor (plus a little protein bonus). You've now got yourself a comforting, wholesome soup that will become part of your regular meal rotation.

¼ cup water

1 tablespoon red miso paste

3 cups Vegetable Broth
(page 112)

2 cups diced onion

1 cup diced carrots

1 cup diced russet potatoes

3 cloves of garlic, minced

½ teaspoon dried basil

½ teaspoon dried oregano

½ teaspoon dried thyme

1 cup chopped frozen or
fresh green beans

1 cup diced tomato

1. In a large saucepan, bring the water to a simmer over medium-high heat. Add the miso and whisk until thick and smooth. Add the broth, onion, carrots, potatoes, garlic, basil, oregano, and thyme, and bring to a boil. Lower the heat to medium-low, cover, and simmer for 10 minutes.

2. Add the green beans and tomato and bring back to a boil. Lower the heat, cover, and simmer for 5 minutes, then serve.

> **FLEX TIP:** For a meat option, try adding chicken meatballs. Take 1 pound of ground chicken seasoned with salt and pepper, and mix with an egg and some bread crumbs so that you can form little meatballs. Bake in the oven at 400°F for about 20 minutes until brown. Add a few meatballs per serving to the soup in step 2. You'll have plenty left over for another meal.

PER SERVING (2 CUPS): Calories: 103; Fat: 1g; Protein: 3g; Carbohydrates: 23g; Fiber: 4g; Sugar: 7g; Sodium: 190mg

Spicy Corn Chowder

FAST FAV. | QUICK PREP.

SERVES: 4 TO 6 | **PREP TIME:** 5 MINUTES | **COOK TIME:** 20 MINUTES

This recipe is the perfect winter soup. It's full of rich, spicy, smoky flavors from the chipotle powder, which adds depth and heat. It is strong, though, so don't use more than the recipe calls for, or your soup might smell like a campfire.

2 medium potatoes, peeled and cut into 1-inch cubes
2 cups Vegetable Broth (page 112)

1 (13½-ounce) can full-fat coconut milk
1 (16-ounce) bag frozen corn
2 tablespoons nutritional yeast

1 teaspoon chipotle powder
1 teaspoon canned diced green chiles, drained
½ teaspoon ground mustard
½ teaspoon paprika

1. In a large pot, combine the potatoes, vegetable broth, coconut milk, corn, nutritional yeast, chipotle powder, green chiles, mustard, and paprika and stir to combine. Bring to a simmer and reduce the heat to medium-low. Cover and simmer for 25 minutes until the potatoes are tender.

2. Remove the soup from the heat and partially blend with a stick blender, or transfer to a blender in small batches and partially blend, leaving some of the soup chunky. Return to the pot and serve.

> **FLEX TIP:** Top your bowls of chowder with crumbled pieces of cooked bacon (about 4 slices) or, for a special occasion, top with ½ cup fresh lobster meat.

PER SERVING: Calories: 385; Fat: 20g; Protein: 8g; Carbohydrates: 48g, Fiber: 6g; Sugar: 1g; Sodium: 144mg

Root Vegetable Soup

FAST FAV. ONE-POT

SERVES: 4 | **PREP TIME:** 10 MINUTES | **COOK TIME:** 20 MINUTES

Fall is the perfect time to serve this filling yet low-calorie, heart-healthy soup. The flavor of the carrots takes center stage, but their sweetness is balanced by the other root vegetables, including a potato that thickens the soup.

1 parsnip, peeled and chopped

1 turnip, peeled and chopped

1 medium onion, chopped

2 or 3 carrots, chopped

2 celery ribs, chopped

1 small potato or ½ russet potato, peeled

1 small leek, white and light green parts, chopped

2 or 3 thyme sprigs

Salt

Freshly ground black pepper

Chopped fresh parsley, for garnish

1. In a large soup pot, combine the parsnip, turnip, onion, carrots, celery, potato, and leek and cover with water by about 2 inches. Bring to a boil over medium-high heat and cook for about 10 minutes, until the vegetables are soft.

2. Using a slotted spoon, transfer the softened vegetables to a food processor or blender, reserving the cooking liquid in the pot. Process until smooth, then return to the pot.

3. Add the thyme sprigs and season with salt and pepper. Bring the mixture back to a boil, reduce the heat to low, and simmer for 10 minutes.

4. Remove the thyme and discard. Top each bowl of soup with a sprinkle of minced parsley.

TIP: You can often find soup starter "kits" in the supermarket's produce section. These kits usually contain a parsnip, a turnip, an onion, a few carrots, and some herbs. Just add a potato for the thickener, and you're all set.

PER SERVING: Calories: 145; Fat: 0g; Protein: 3g; Carbohydrates: 34g, Fiber: 5g; Sugar: 6g; Sodium: 98mg

Asparagus and Leek Soup

ONE-POT

SERVES: 4 | **PREP TIME:** 15 MINUTES | **COOK TIME:** 35 MINUTES

This protein- and fiber-rich soup is a delicious use of seasonal vegetables. Asparagus is typically served as a side dish, but it deserves to be the star, thanks to its unique savory flavor and nutritional benefits.

2 leeks, white and light green parts, halved lengthwise, thinly sliced, and thoroughly washed
1 tablespoon water
2 cloves of garlic, minced

¾ teaspoon dried tarragon (or dried dill or thyme)
1 cup dried red lentils
1 pound asparagus, cut into 1-inch pieces, including the ends

6 cups Vegetable Broth (page 112)
Juice of 1 lemon
Freshly ground black pepper

1. In a large pot over medium-high heat, combine the leeks and water, and sauté for 5 minutes. Add the garlic and tarragon, and sauté for 2 minutes.

2. Add the lentils, asparagus, and vegetable broth. Bring the soup to a boil, cover, reduce the heat to medium-low, and simmer for 20 to 30 minutes, until the lentils are tender.

3. Remove some of the cooked lentils, leeks, and asparagus if you'd like some larger pieces in your soup. Using an immersion blender, puree the soup until smooth, or slightly chunky if preferred. Stir in the reserved ingredients if using.

4. Serve with a drizzle of fresh lemon juice and season with pepper.

FLEX TIP: In addition to the fresh lemon juice and black pepper, try garnishing your soup with a drizzle of sour cream or crème fraiche, or even some herbed goat cheese.

PER SERVING: Calories: 237; Fat: 1g; Protein: 15g; Carbohydrates: 45g, Fiber: 8g; Sugar: 4g; Sodium: 115mg

Coconut Curry Ramen

FAST FAV. **ONE-POT**

SERVES: 4 | **PREP TIME:** 10 MINUTES | **COOK TIME:** 15 MINUTES

Instant ramen noodles get a grown-up makeover in this soupy noodle dish, though you can swap them for healthier spiralized zucchini noodles. The heat from Thai red curry paste is balanced perfectly with creamy coconut milk and the bright acidity of lime. Try topping this with red cabbage because the color is a great contrast with the orange-hued soup, and it adds a nice texture, but if you don't like cabbage, chunks of avocado would be just as delicious.

---

2 to 3 tablespoons Thai red curry paste

2 teaspoons peeled and grated fresh ginger

1 teaspoon minced garlic

2 baby bok choy heads, coarsely chopped

6 cremini mushrooms, stems removed and caps sliced

1 (13½-ounce) can full-fat coconut milk

1 cup snow peas, halved

⅔ cup Vegetable Broth (page 112)

4 (3-ounce) packages instant ramen noodles (seasoning packets discarded)

3 cups shredded red cabbage

1 lime, quartered, for garnish

1. In a large pot, heat the curry paste, ginger, and garlic over medium heat for 2 minutes, until fragrant. Add the bok choy, mushrooms, coconut milk, snow peas, and vegetable broth and bring to a simmer. Cook for 10 minutes.

2. Add the ramen noodles to the pot and cook for another 3 minutes, tossing the ramen until coated.

3. Divide into bowls, top with the shredded cabbage, and serve with lime wedges.

FLEX TIP: Soft-boiled eggs make a nice addition to ramen. Place 4 eggs in a saucepan large enough so they sit in a single layer. Fill the pan with enough cold water to cover the eggs completely. Bring to a boil. Turn off the heat and let them stand for 2 to 3 minutes. Gently peel before adding one egg to each bowl of ramen. For a medium egg, let stand for 5 minutes.

PER SERVING: Calories: 596; Fat: 32g; Protein: 9g; Carbohydrates: 68g, Fiber: 7g; Sugar: 9g; Sodium: 241mg

Minestrone with Beans

ONE-POT

SERVES: 4 TO 6 | **PREP TIME**: 10 MINUTES | **COOK TIME**: 40 MINUTES

Minestrone is a vegetable soup from Italy that is usually made with pasta. Here we are adding beans to make the soup even heartier and topping each bowl with a dollop of pesto for an added fresh flavor. This soup reheats well and tastes even better the next day.

2 tablespoons extra-virgin olive oil

1 small onion, chopped

2 carrots, chopped

2 celery ribs, chopped

2 cloves of garlic, minced

2 cups loosely packed Swiss chard or spinach, stems trimmed, leaves chopped

2 russet potatoes, peeled and cut into 1-inch cubes

1 (14½-ounce) can diced tomatoes

1 (15-ounce) can cannellini beans, drained and rinsed

4 cups Vegetable Broth (page 112)

1 teaspoon salt

½ teaspoon freshly ground black pepper

1 cup small pasta, such as ditalini (small tubular pasta) or orzo (rice-shaped pasta)

2 tablespoons Plant Pesto (page 113)

1. Heat the olive oil in a large stockpot over medium heat. Add the onion, carrots, celery, and garlic. Cook for 5 minutes until the onion starts to soften.

2. Add the Swiss chard, potatoes, and tomatoes. Cook for about 10 minutes, until the chard wilts and the tomatoes start to break down.

3. Add the beans, broth, salt, and pepper. Bring to a boil, and simmer for 15 minutes until potatoes are soft.

4. Add the pasta, and cook until al dente, about 10 minutes.

5. Top each bowl of soup with a teaspoon of pesto and serve.

FLEX TIP: In step 1, add 4 ounces of diced pancetta or bacon for an extra smoky flavor.

PER SERVING: Calories: 420; Fat: 12g; Protein: 14g; Carbohydrates: 66g; Fiber: 12g; Sugar: 7g; Sodium: 853mg

Vegetable and Lentil Stew

ONE-POT

SERVES: 4 | **PREP TIME**: 10 MINUTES | **COOK TIME**: 40 MINUTES

Is there anything more comforting than a bowl of chunky stew served with crusty bread? The lentils add a rich thickness to this meal. Be sure to cut the vegetables into chunky pieces.

1 small onion, chopped
2 cloves of garlic, minced
1 cup carrots, sliced into
   ½-inch rounds
3 celery ribs, sliced
3 large russet potatoes, cut
   into 1-inch pieces

1 teaspoon salt
½ teaspoon freshly ground
   black pepper
4 cups Vegetable Broth
   (page 112)
½ cup lentils
1 tablespoon Dijon mustard

1 teaspoon fresh thyme
   leaves
½ cup frozen peas

1. In a large stockpot, combine the onion, garlic, carrots, celery, potatoes, salt, and pepper. Add the broth and bring to a boil over medium-high heat.

2. Stir in the lentils, mustard, and thyme. Cover and let simmer for 30 minutes until the lentils are tender.

3. Add the peas and cook uncovered for 5 minutes.

FLEX TIP: For a beef stew, brown 1 pound of stewing beef in a little olive oil and a teaspoon of white vinegar for 8 to 10 minutes before step 1. Leave in the pot and continue with the rest of the directions.

PER SERVING: Calories: 347; Fat: 1g; Protein: 14g; Carbohydrates: 74g; Fiber: 9g; Sugar: 6g; Sodium: 688mg

Pea and Zucchini Soup

ONE-POT

SERVES: 4 | **PREP TIME:** 10 MINUTES | **COOK TIME:** 30 MINUTES

This beautiful soup has a vivid green color and fresh summery flavor. The potato acts as a thickener in place of cream, significantly reducing the calories.

3 zucchini, cut into 1-inch cubes

1 russet potato, peeled, and cut into 1-inch cubes

1 small onion, chopped

3 cups Vegetable Broth (page 112)

½ teaspoon salt

2 cups frozen peas

2 cloves of garlic, minced

1 teaspoon lemon zest

Extra-virgin olive oil, for drizzling

1 tablespoon chopped fresh mint

½ teaspoon freshly ground black pepper

1. In a large stockpot, place the zucchini, potato, onion, vegetable broth, and salt. Cover and bring to a boil over medium-high heat. Lower the heat and simmer for 15 minutes until the potatoes are soft.

2. Add the peas, and simmer for another 3 minutes, until the peas thaw.

3. Using a slotted spoon, transfer the softened vegetables to a food processor or blender, reserving the cooking liquid in the pot. Process the vegetables until smooth, then return to the pot. You could also use a stick blender for this step.

4. Add the garlic and lemon zest. Stir to combine. Bring the mixture back up to a boil, then reduce the heat and simmer for 10 minutes.

5. Top each bowl of soup with a drizzle of olive oil, a sprinkle of fresh mint, and black pepper.

FLEX TIP: For an added meat option, include 4 ounces of chopped cooked ham in step 4. Ham perfectly complements the flavor of peas.

PER SERVING: Calories: 166; Fat: 1g; Protein: 8g; Carbohydrates: 34g, Fiber: 7g; Sugar: 9g; Sodium: 312mg

Smoky Eggplant and Yellow Squash Soup

QUICK PREP.

SERVES: 4 | **PREP TIME:** 5 MINUTES | **COOK TIME:** 40 MINUTES

This vegetable soup gets its smoky flavor from smoked paprika and ground cumin. This recipe makes a thick, chunky vegetable soup. If you want a smooth, creamy soup, use an immersion blender right before serving.

1 eggplant, cut into 1-inch cubes

2 yellow squash, cut into 1-inch cubes

1 red bell pepper, seeded, cut into 1-inch cubes

1 large onion, chopped

¼ cup extra-virgin olive oil

½ teaspoon salt

¼ teaspoon freshly ground black pepper

1 (15-ounce) can diced tomatoes, undrained

6 cloves of garlic, minced

1 tablespoon smoked paprika

1 teaspoon ground cumin

6 cups Vegetable Broth (page 112)

¼ cup chopped fresh flat-leaf parsley for garnish

1. Preheat the oven to 450°F. Prepare a rimmed baking sheet with nonstick cooking spray.

2. In a large bowl, combine the eggplant, yellow squash, red bell pepper, and onion. Add the olive oil, salt, and pepper, and toss to coat. Arrange on the baking sheet and bake for 30 minutes until the vegetables are soft and browned around the edges.

3. In a stockpot, add the tomatoes, garlic, smoked paprika, and cumin. Add the roasted vegetables and vegetable broth. Bring to a boil over medium-high heat. Reduce to a simmer and cook for 10 minutes until all the flavors combine.

4. Top each bowl with a sprinkle of parsley as garnish.

FLEX TIP: Add 1 pound of Spanish or Mexican chorizo cut into coins to the soup pot with a little olive oil and cook through before adding the tomatoes in step 3.

PER SERVING: Calories: 225; Fat: 15g; Protein: 5g; Carbohydrates: 23g, Fiber: 9g; Sugar: 13g; Sodium: 426mg

Spinach Orzo Soup

ONE-POT

SERVES: 4 TO 6 | **PREP TIME**: 10 MINUTES | **COOK TIME**: 25 MINUTES

This colorful soup makes a perfect meal on a chilly evening. Orzo is a tiny pasta that is shaped like rice kernels. For the cold and flu season, follow the Flex Tip for a healing bowl of comfort.

2 tablespoons extra-virgin olive oil

1 small onion, finely chopped

1 cup finely chopped carrots

1 cup finely chopped celery

4 cloves of garlic, minced

8 cups Vegetable Broth (page 112)

1 (14½-ounce) can diced fire-roasted tomatoes

1 teaspoon salt

½ teaspoon freshly ground black pepper

Pinch red pepper flakes

1½ cups orzo

4 cups fresh baby spinach leaves, stems removed

1. Heat the oil in a large stockpot over medium-high heat. Add the onion and cook for about 5 minutes until it starts to soften. Add the carrots, celery, and garlic, and sauté for 5 minutes, until soft.

2. Add the broth, tomatoes, salt, black pepper, and red pepper flakes, and bring to a boil.

3. Add the orzo and let simmer for 10 minutes, until the pasta is al dente.

4. Add the spinach, and cook for an additional 5 minutes, until the spinach has wilted.

FLEX TIP: Make this soup with chicken broth and add 1 pound of shredded cooked chicken or tiny chicken meatballs. You can replace the orzo with cheese-filled tortellini for an even heartier dish.

PER SERVING: Calories: 357; Fat: 8g; Protein: 11g; Carbohydrates: 61g, Fiber: 8g; Sugar: 6g; Sodium: 780mg

Potato Leek Soup

ONE-POT

SERVES: 4 | **PREP TIME:** 10 MINUTES | **COOK TIME:** 40 MINUTES

This recipe is a lightened-up version of a classic French soup called *vichyssoise*. This soup is just as delicious as the original and easy to make with a few ingredient tweaks. I like to serve this soup with simple rosemary croutons for a bit of crunch. The croutons can be made ahead and stored in an airtight container at room temperature for up to one week.

FOR THE SOUP

2 tablespoons extra-virgin olive oil

2 large leeks, sliced, white and light green parts only, rinsed well

2 cloves of garlic, minced

4 large russet potatoes, peeled and cut into 1-inch pieces

4 cups Vegetable Broth (page 112)

1½ cups water

1 teaspoon salt

½ teaspoon freshly ground black pepper

FOR THE ROSEMARY CROUTONS

4 stale French bread slices, cut into cubes

3 tablespoons extra-virgin olive oil

½ teaspoon minced fresh rosemary

TO MAKE THE SOUP

1. In a stockpot, heat the oil on medium heat and sauté the leeks and garlic until the leeks are soft, about 8 minutes.

2. Add the potatoes, broth, and water, and bring to a boil.

3. Reduce the heat to a simmer and cook with the lid on for 30 minutes, stirring occasionally, until the potatoes are soft and falling apart.

4. Remove from the heat. With a potato masher, break up the potatoes. Add the salt and pepper and stir. You should have a thick, chunky consistency. If you want a smoother soup, you can use a stick blender.

TO MAKE THE ROSEMARY CROUTONS

5. While the soup is simmering, preheat the oven to 400°F. Line a rimmed baking sheet with parchment paper.

6. In a large bowl, toss the bread cubes with olive oil and rosemary. Spread out on the prepared sheet and bake for about 10 minutes, until brown and crisp. Transfer the croutons to a plate lined with paper towels.

7. Divide the soup into serving bowls and top each serving with rosemary croutons.

FLEX TIP: The traditional French version uses butter and chicken broth. Heavy cream is added at the end. You can make a vegan heavy cream by combining ½ block of silken tofu (about 6 ounces) with ½ cup of your favorite plant-based milk in a blender.

PER SERVING: Calories: 472; Fat: 12g; Protein: 11g; Carbohydrates: 82g, Fiber: 6g; Sugar: 5g; Sodium: 595mg

Easy Gazpacho

FAST FAV. | ONE-POT

SERVES: 4 | **PREP TIME:** 15 MINUTES

Gazpacho is a chilled soup from southern Spain that might remind you of a zesty tomato smoothie. It helps keep you cool on a hot summer day, and it's packed with veggies for nutrition. Serve it in a wine glass for a beautiful presentation.

2 cups chopped fresh tomatoes

1½ cups diced cucumber

½ cup chopped sweet yellow onion

½ red bell pepper, diced

10 or 12 fresh basil leaves

2 cloves of garlic

¼ cup extra-virgin olive oil

2 tablespoons red wine vinegar

½ teaspoon salt

¼ teaspoon freshly ground black pepper

1. Place the tomatoes, cucumber, onion, bell pepper, basil, garlic, olive oil, vinegar, salt, and pepper in a blender, and puree until smooth. Reserve 2 tablespoons of the cucumber and bell pepper for garnish.

2. Refrigerate for 30 minutes before serving for the best flavor.

3. To serve, pour into bowls or wine glasses. Garnish with diced cucumber and red bell pepper.

FLEX TIP: This soup is lovely topped with a couple tablespoons of chopped smoked salmon and a dollop of sour cream.

PER SERVING: Calories: 166; Fat: 14g; Protein: 2g; Carbohydrates: 10g, Fiber: 2g; Sugar: 5g; Sodium: 300mg

Southwest Stuffed Peppers ◆ 82

CHAPTER 6

Entrées

Southwest Stuffed Peppers ◆ 82

Hearty Chickpea Burgers ◆ 83

Burst Cherry Tomato Rigatoni ◆ 84

Red Curry Vegetables ◆ 85

Egg-Roll-in-a-Bowl Stir-Fry ◆ 86

Vegan Lasagna ◆ 87

Kebabs with Spicy Peanut Sauce ◆ 89

Gnocchi Puttanesca ◆ 91

Potato and Leek Pie ◆ 92

Spaghetti with Olive Oil, Garlic, and Olives ◆ 93

Portobello Steaks with Spinach and Polenta ◆ 94

Vegetable Paella ◆ 96

Baked Falafel Bowl ◆ 98

Southwest Stuffed Peppers

SERVES: 4 | **PREP TIME:** 10 MINUTES | **COOK TIME:** 30 MINUTES

Stuffed peppers are great if you're looking for a delicious, easy dinner that also stores well for leftovers. Red or yellow bell peppers will impart a bit more flavor to the dish. To kick the heat up, add a few slices of jalapeño pepper into the rice mixture before filling the bell peppers.

4 bell peppers (any color), tops cut off and seeded

3 cups cooked brown rice

1 cup cooked black beans

1 cup corn (fresh or frozen)

1 cup Vegetable Broth (page 112)

2 tablespoons tomato paste

2 tablespoons chili powder

1 teaspoon ground cumin

1. Preheat the oven to 375°F.

2. In a large bowl, mix the rice, beans, corn, broth, tomato paste, chili powder, and cumin until the tomato paste and spices are thoroughly incorporated.

3. Spoon one-quarter of the rice mixture into each pepper. Set the peppers upright on a 9-inch-square baking dish and place the tops back onto the peppers.

4. Bake for 30 minutes, or until the peppers are easily pierced with a fork, and serve.

> **FLEX TIP:** You can add 1 pound of ground beef or turkey to the stuffing mixture but reduce the brown rice to 2 cups and leave out the beans. Before adding to the mixture, cook the meat separately in a large skillet on medium heat until browned and fully cooked.

PER SERVING: Calories: 270; Fat: 3g; Protein: 11g; Carbohydrates: 55g, Fiber: 9g; Sugar: 8g; Sodium: 133mg

Hearty Chickpea Burgers

FAST FAV.

SERVES: 4 | **PREP TIME:** 15 MINUTES | **COOK TIME:** 10 MINUTES

These walnut and chickpea burgers will satisfy everyone with their rich umami flavors, juicy interior, and 11 grams of protein per patty. Serve them on a hearty wheat bun with slices of tomatoes, lettuce, vegan mayo, and any other toppings you enjoy.

2 tablespoons ground flaxseed

¼ cup water

1 cup raw walnuts

½ cup whole wheat bread crumbs or gluten-free bread crumbs

1 clove of garlic, peeled and stemmed

1 teaspoon chili powder

1 teaspoon smoked paprika

½ teaspoon garlic powder

¼ teaspoon onion powder

¾ cup canned chickpeas, drained and rinsed

3 tablespoons peanut butter

1 tablespoon apple cider vinegar

Nonstick cooking spray

1. In a small bowl, whisk together the flaxseed and water. Set aside for 10 minutes to gel.

2. In a food processor, combine the walnuts, bread crumbs, garlic, chili powder, paprika, garlic powder, and onion powder. Process for about 2 minutes until crumbly. Add the soaked flaxseed, chickpeas, peanut butter, and vinegar. Process for 1 to 2 minutes, or until fully combined.

3. Transfer the mixture to a large bowl and knead for 1 to 2 minutes, or until the mixture comes together. Divide the dough into 4 equal parts and shape into ½-inch-thick patties.

4. Generously spray a large nonstick skillet with cooking spray, and cook the patties over medium heat for 3 to 5 minutes per side until browned and crispy. Serve immediately.

TIP: These burgers should be cooked in a skillet before trying to grill them. Once cooked, they hold together well and can be transferred to a hot grill for a little char.

PER SERVING: Calories: 338; Fat: 25g; Protein: 13g; Carbohydrates: 22g; Fiber: 7g; Sugar: 5g; Sodium: 174mg

Burst Cherry Tomato Rigatoni

FAST FAV. | **QUICK PREP.**

SERVES: 4 | **PREP TIME:** 5 MINUTES | **COOK TIME:** 15 MINUTES

This is a great dish when farmers' markets are bursting with fresh tomatoes, but if you find yourself craving it midwinter, canned whole cherry tomatoes work as well; just reduce your cooking time slightly.

1 (16-ounce) box whole wheat rigatoni or similar tube-shaped pasta

3 tablespoons grapeseed or extra-virgin olive oil

4 cloves of garlic, thinly sliced

Zest of ½ lemon

½ teaspoon red pepper flakes

¼ teaspoon salt

3 pints whole cherry tomatoes or 3 (14-ounce) cans whole cherry tomatoes, drained

¼ cup chopped fresh basil

3 tablespoons nutritional yeast or vegan Parmesan cheese

1. Bring a large pot of water to a boil over high heat and cook the pasta according to package directions.

2. While the pasta is cooking, in a large skillet, heat the oil over medium heat. Add the garlic, lemon zest, red pepper flakes, and salt. Sauté until the garlic is light brown.

3. Add the cherry tomatoes and reduce the heat to low. Cook until the tomatoes blister and soften, about 6 minutes. Use a fork or potato masher to mash about one-third of the tomatoes gently.

4. Drain the pasta, reserving 1 cup of pasta water. Add the pasta to the skillet, along with ¼ cup of the pasta water, and toss. Continue adding the pasta water in ¼-cup increments until all the pasta is coated (it's okay if you don't use all the water). Top with the basil and nutritional yeast, and serve.

FLEX TIP: Elevate this dish by adding zucchini slices and chopped onions to the skillet with the garlic or crumbling in 1 hot Italian sausage for its spicy flavor. For a dairy option, replace the nutritional yeast with grated Parmesan cheese.

PER SERVING: Calories: 555; Fat: 14g; Protein: 20g; Carbohydrates: 104g, Fiber: 15g; Sugar: 7g; Sodium: 532mg

Red Curry Vegetables

FAST FAV. | QUICK PREP.

SERVES: 4 | **PREP TIME:** 5 MINUTES | **COOK TIME:** 15 MINUTES

This dish is healthier than takeout! Use frozen stir-fry vegetable mixes to add a variety of vegetables and reduce the prep time. I like serving this over homemade coconut rice, which you can easily make by using a regular jasmine rice recipe and swapping 1 cup of water for 1 cup of full-fat coconut milk plus 1 tablespoon of sugar.

1 tablespoon extra-virgin olive oil

1 medium onion, diced

1 clove of garlic, minced

1 teaspoon peeled and grated fresh ginger

1 (16-ounce) bag frozen stir-fry vegetables

1 (13½-ounce) can full-fat coconut milk

½ cup Vegetable Broth (page 112)

1 tablespoon Thai red curry paste

2 teaspoons cold water

1 teaspoon cornstarch

1. In a large skillet, heat the oil on medium-high heat. Add the onion and cook for about 5 minutes until translucent. Add the garlic and ginger and cook, stirring constantly, for 30 seconds, until fragrant. Add the frozen vegetables and stir to combine.

2. Pour in the coconut milk, vegetable broth, and curry paste, and bring to a simmer. Cook for 7 to 10 minutes, until the vegetables are fork-tender.

3. In a small bowl, mix the water and cornstarch. Add the cornstarch slurry to the pan and stir continuously for 1 minute or until the sauce thickens. Serve.

FLEX TIP: Curry dishes are adaptable to many protein additions. Try sautéing 16 ounces of white meat chicken breast cubes or peeled shrimp before adding the onion in step 1.

PER SERVING: Calories: 328; Fat: 27g; Protein: 6g; Carbohydrates: 20g, Fiber: 5g; Sugar: 1g; Sodium: 87mg

Egg-Roll-in-a-Bowl Stir-Fry

FAST FAV.   QUICK PREP.

SERVES: 4 | **PREP TIME:** 5 MINUTES | **COOK TIME:** 15 MINUTES

This dish has all the classic flavors of an egg roll but without the deep-frying or the wrapper. It's delicious as a meal on its own or as a filling for lettuce wraps. I've used tempeh to add protein, but you could swap it out for tofu if you prefer. You could also add some slivered snow peas or water chestnuts for more crunch.

2 tablespoons canola or grapeseed oil, divided

1 (7-ounce) package tempeh, crumbled

1 large onion, diced

1 (10-ounce) bag shredded cabbage

2 cups shredded carrots

¼ cup tamari or dark soy sauce

2 tablespoons sesame oil

1 tablespoon peeled and grated fresh ginger

2 teaspoons minced garlic

½ teaspoon freshly ground black pepper

1. In a large skillet, heat 1 tablespoon of canola oil on medium-high heat. Add the tempeh and onion and cook for 4 minutes, until the onion is just translucent.

2. Reduce the heat to medium and add the cabbage and carrots. Cook for 4 minutes, stirring occasionally.

3. While the vegetables are cooking, in a small bowl, whisk together the tamari, sesame oil, ginger, garlic, and pepper and the remaining 1 tablespoon of oil.

4. Pour the sauce over the cabbage mixture in the pan and toss well to coat. Continue cooking for 5 to 10 minutes, or until the cabbage is tender, and serve.

> **FLEX TIP:** Instead of tempeh, there are several options for adding meat to your bowls—1 pound of ground turkey, beef, or pork, or sautéed shrimp would all be delicious.

PER SERVING: Calories: 285; Fat: 10g; Protein: 13g; Carbohydrates: 18g; Fiber: 6g; Sugar: 7g; Sodium: 1063mg

Vegan Lasagna

QUICK PREP.

SERVES: 4 | **PREP TIME:** 5 MINUTES | **COOK TIME:** 40 MINUTES

Lasagna is a layered casserole from Italy made of pasta, sauce, and usually cheese. They often use ricotta cheese in southern Italy, although the lasagna is usually made with béchamel sauce in northern Italy. Both versions are creamy and delicious. Lasagna freezes well if you want to double-batch this and save one for another time.

---

1 (16-ounce) box lasagna noodles

1 onion, roughly chopped

2 carrots, roughly chopped

2 celery ribs, roughly chopped

1 zucchini, roughly chopped

4 portobello mushrooms, roughly chopped

1 red bell pepper, seeded and roughly chopped

2 cloves of garlic

2 tablespoons extra-virgin olive oil

1 tablespoon dried oregano

1 teaspoon salt

½ teaspoon freshly ground black pepper

¼ teaspoon red pepper flakes

2 cups Basic Tomato Basil Sauce (page 115)

2 cups Vegan Béchamel (page 117)

1 cup shredded vegan cheese

1. Preheat the oven to 425°F. In a pot of salted boiling water, cook the lasagna noodles for half of their recommended cooking time. They should start to soften but not cook through. Remove from the water, and pat dry with paper towels.

2. While the pasta cooks, place the onion, carrot, celery, zucchini, mushrooms, bell pepper, and garlic in a food processor, and pulse a few times to create a chunky pulp.

3. In a large skillet, heat the olive oil over medium-high heat. Transfer the vegetable mixture to the skillet and add the oregano, salt, black pepper, and red pepper flakes, and sauté for 10 minutes until the veggies are softened.

4. In a 2-quart casserole dish (11-by-7-by-1½-inch), spoon in a layer of tomato sauce. Place a layer of lasagna noodles on top. Spoon half of the vegetable mixture on top. (Use a slotted spoon so that the vegetables are not too wet.) Pour on 1 cup of the Béchamel sauce. Then dollop on more of the tomato sauce, but not too much. You don't want this to be too wet.

CONTINUED

5. Add another layer of lasagna noodles, the rest of the vegetable mixture, and another cup of Béchamel sauce.

6. Top with another layer of lasagna noodles and a light coating of tomato sauce. Top with a layer of shredded vegan cheese.

7. Cover the dish with foil and bake for 20 minutes. Remove foil and cook for another 10 minutes, or until the cheese is brown and bubbly.

FLEX TIP: This vegetable mixture is meant to replace ground beef. If you want to make a traditional lasagna, substitute 1 pound of seasoned ground beef for the vegetables and top the dish with a shredded Italian cheese blend.

PER SERVING: Calories: 582; Fat: 22g; Protein: 13g; Carbohydrates: 81g; Fiber: 10g; Sugar: 19g; Sodium: 970mg

Kebabs with Spicy Peanut Sauce

FAST FAV.

SERVES: 4 TO 6 | **PREP TIME:** 15 MINUTES | **COOK TIME:** 15 MINUTES

Roasted vegetables taste even better when marinated. This lime-based marinade perfectly complements the citrus in the spicy peanut sauce. Serve these kebabs at your next barbecue. These also cook up well on a grill.

FOR THE MARINADE

½ cup extra-virgin olive oil

Juice of 2 limes

4 cloves of garlic, minced

1 teaspoon dried oregano

½ teaspoon salt

¼ teaspoon freshly ground black pepper

¼ teaspoon red pepper flakes

FOR THE KEBABS

1 zucchini, cut into 1-inch rounds

1 yellow squash, cut into 1-inch rounds

2 cups whole button mushrooms

1 onion, white or red, cut into eighths and halved lengthwise

1 red or orange bell pepper, cut into 1-inch pieces

1 green bell pepper, cut into 1-inch pieces

1 cup cherry tomatoes

2 cups Spicy Peanut Sauce (page 118)

1. Preheat the oven to 400°F. Line a baking sheet with foil and spray it with nonstick cooking spray.

2. In a large bowl, whisk together the olive oil, lime juice, garlic, oregano, salt, black pepper, and red pepper flakes. Add the vegetables, toss gently to coat, and allow them to marinate for at least 10 minutes.

3. Thread the vegetables onto skewers, making sure each skewer receives equal amounts. Place the skewers onto the baking sheet.

CONTINUED

4. Cook for 10 to 15 minutes, until vegetables are cooked through and starting to brown around the edges.

5. Serve with peanut sauce on the side for dipping.

FLEX TIP: Add whole shrimp, salmon, or swordfish cut into 1-inch cubes for a seafood option. For chicken, boneless skinless thighs work well. For a red meat option, try chunks of stewing beef or even meatballs.

PER SERVING: Calories: 374; Fat: 31g; Protein: 12g; Carbohydrates: 25g, Fiber: 8g; Sugar: 12g; Sodium: 151mg

Gnocchi Puttanesca

FAST FAV. **QUICK PREP.**

SERVES: 4 | **PREP TIME:** 5 MINUTES | **COOK TIME:** 25 MINUTES

Gnocchi are little pasta dumplings made with potatoes. Puttanesca is a highly flavorful tomato sauce that originated in Naples, Italy. It's delicious on any pasta and works especially well on gnocchi.

---

2 tablespoons extra-virgin olive oil

4 cloves of garlic, minced

1 (6-ounce) can tomato paste

½ cup water

1 (28-ounce) can crushed tomatoes

½ cup pitted Kalamata olives

1 tablespoon capers

1 teaspoon dried oregano

½ teaspoon salt

¼ teaspoon freshly ground black pepper

¼ teaspoon red pepper flakes

1 (17-ounce) package gnocchi

¼ cup chopped fresh basil leaves for garnish

1. Warm the oil in a large saucepan over medium heat. Add the garlic and cook for 1 minute until fragrant.

2. Add the tomato paste and cook for 1 minute, stirring. Add the water and stir until the tomato paste melts into the water.

3. Add the crushed tomatoes, olives, capers, oregano, salt, black pepper, and red pepper flakes, and stir to combine.

4. Bring the sauce to a boil, then reduce the heat to a low simmer and cook for 20 minutes, partially covered.

5. In the meantime, in a large pot of boiling salted water, cook the gnocchi according to the package instructions, usually 2 to 5 minutes, until they start to float.

6. Drain the gnocchi and serve topped with Puttanesca sauce and fresh basil.

> **FLEX TIP:** For a seafood option, add 4 anchovy fillets to the sauce at the same time as the garlic. They will melt and add a wonderful briny flavor. Baked or grilled tuna steaks and salmon fillets work well with the Puttanesca sauce. Serve on the side.

PER SERVING: Calories: 344; Fat: 17g; Protein: 8g; Carbohydrates: 45g; Fiber: 8g; Sugar: 15g; Sodium: 920mg

Potato and Leek Pie

SERVES: 4 | **PREP TIME:** 10 MINUTES | **COOK TIME:** 60 MINUTES

2 large potatoes, peeled and cut into ¼-inch slices

2 tablespoons extra-virgin olive oil

2 leeks, white and light green parts only, sliced and rinsed well

1 onion, chopped

¼ teaspoon salt

¼ teaspoon white pepper

Pinch nutmeg

⅓ cup water

2 teaspoons Dijon mustard

½ cup Vegan Béchamel (page 117), divided

2 store-bought vegan pie crusts

1 tablespoon almond milk

½ teaspoon salt

1. Preheat the oven to 375°F. Prepare a 9-inch pie pan by spraying it with nonstick cooking spray.

2. In a medium saucepan over high heat, bring the potatoes to a boil in salted water, reduce the heat to low, and simmer for 10 minutes, until just tender. Drain and set aside.

3. In a large skillet, heat the olive oil over medium heat. Add the leeks, onion, salt, white pepper, and nutmeg. Cook, stirring, for 10 minutes, until softened.

4. Add the water and cook until most of it has evaporated. Stir in the mustard and set aside to cool.

5. Arrange one of the pie crusts in the pie pan. Spoon in half of the leek mixture, pour on ¼ cup of the béchamel sauce, and top with a layer of potatoes. Press down with the back of a spoon to compact everything.

6. Add the remaining leek mixture, Béchamel sauce, and potatoes.

7. Top with the second pie crust, crimping together the edges to seal it shut.

8. Brush the top of the pie with the almond milk, cut a few slits in the lid to vent, and sprinkle with salt.

9. Bake for 45 to 50 minutes, or until golden. Allow to rest for 10 minutes before serving.

FLEX TIP: Use a pie crust made with butter and brush the top with an egg wash.

PER SERVING: Calories: 663; Fat: 31g; Protein: 11g; Carbohydrates: 85g; Fiber: 8g; Sugar: 8g; Sodium: 868mg

Spaghetti with Olive Oil, Garlic, and Olives

FAST FAV.

SERVES: 4 | **PREP TIME**: 10 MINUTES | **COOK TIME**: 10 MINUTES

This meal is pure Italian comfort food, and it all comes together in the time it takes to boil the pasta. This recipe is also conducive to creative and seasonal variations. Try adding zucchini in the summertime or broccoli in winter.

1 pound spaghetti
½ cup extra-virgin olive oil
6 cloves of garlic, minced
¼ teaspoon red pepper flakes

12 or 15 pitted Kalamata olives, chopped
½ teaspoon dried oregano
½ teaspoon salt

¼ teaspoon freshly ground black pepper
¼ cup chopped fresh basil leaves

1. Bring a large pot of salted water to boil over high heat. Add the spaghetti and cook according to the package instructions until al dente, 9 to 11 minutes.

2. In the meantime, in a large skillet, warm the olive oil, garlic, and red pepper flakes over low heat. The flavors will infuse the olive oil. Be careful not to let the garlic brown, or it can taste bitter.

3. When the pasta is nearly ready, add the olives, oregano, salt, and pepper to the olive oil mixture. Warm them in the olive oil; no need to cook them.

4. Drain the spaghetti, reserving ½ cup of the cooking water.

5. Add the spaghetti to the skillet and toss to combine. Add the basil and a little of the pasta water to create a silkiness. Toss thoroughly and serve.

> **FLEX TIP:** Sprinkle the top with grated Parmesan cheese. This recipe works well with a can of tuna or mackerel packed in olive oil. Drain and add at the same time as the olives in step 3.

PER SERVING: Calories: 687; Fat: 20g; Protein: 15g; Carbohydrates: 87g, Fiber: 4g; Sugar: 3g; Sodium: 482mg

Portobello Steaks with Spinach and Polenta

SERVES: 4 | **PREP TIME:** 15 MINUTES | **COOK TIME:** 30 MINUTES

Portobello mushrooms are a worthy substitute for beef in most scenarios. They are big, hearty, and hold up well to roasting and grilling. This meal is comforting and wholesome. It includes a whole grain, leafy greens, and lots of delicious mushroom gravy. Serve with a crusty baguette.

FOR THE STEAKS

2 tablespoons extra-virgin olive oil

1 tablespoon balsamic vinegar

2 cloves of garlic, minced

Pinch salt

Pinch freshly ground black pepper

4 large portobello mushrooms, stems trimmed

1 (16-ounce) bag frozen spinach, thawed and drained

½ cup water

1 cup instant polenta

2 tablespoons vegan butter

FOR THE MUSHROOM GRAVY

¼ cup water

1 (16-ounce) package sliced mushrooms (white or cremini)

2 shallots, finely chopped

2 tablespoons vegan butter

¼ cup all-purpose flour

3 cups mushroom broth or Vegetable Broth (page 112)

1 tablespoon soy sauce

½ teaspoon salt

¼ teaspoon freshly ground black pepper

1 rosemary sprig

TO MAKE THE STEAKS

1. Preheat the oven to 400°F.

2. Whisk the oil, vinegar, garlic, salt, and pepper in a small bowl.

3. Arrange the mushrooms in a large 3-quart baking dish (9-by-13-by-2-inch) top-side down. Pour the marinade over the mushrooms and cook for 20 minutes. Flip and cook for 5 to 10 minutes until the mushrooms are cooked all the way through.

4. In the meantime, place the frozen spinach in a large saucepan or skillet with the water and cook over low heat, until warmed through, about 5 minutes.

5. In a saucepan, prepare the polenta according to the package directions. It should take about 5 minutes. Stir in the vegan butter.

TO MAKE THE MUSHROOM GRAVY

6. In a large saucepan, heat water with the sliced mushrooms, shallot, and butter over medium heat. The mushrooms will release their juices. Cook until the liquid is almost evaporated, stirring occasionally, about 15 minutes.

7. Add the flour and stir until the mushrooms are coated.

8. Slowly add the broth 1 cup at a time, whisking to incorporate and smooth out any lumps. Season with soy sauce, salt, pepper, and the rosemary sprig. Simmer over medium heat for 15 minutes, stirring often. The gravy will start to thicken. Discard the rosemary before serving.

9. Divide the polenta evenly among 4 plates. Smooth it out flat. Top with a quarter of the spinach. Place 1 portobello mushroom on top and drizzle the mushroom gravy over the whole dish.

> **FLEX TIP:** The polenta, spinach, and mushroom gravy go very well with filet mignon or steak. For a meat dinner, replace the portobello with steak or keep both the mushroom and the steak. The mushroom gravy can be made in advance and refrigerated for up to 3 days. Simply reheat on medium-low before using.

PER SERVING: Calories: 417; Fat: 20g; Protein: 14g; Carbohydrates: 52g; Fiber: 7g; Sugar: 6g; Sodium: 614mg

Vegetable Paella

ONE-POT

SERVES: 4 | **PREP TIME:** 15 MINUTES | **COOK TIME:** 1 HOUR, 15 MINUTES

Paella is a rice dish from Spain that is usually cooked outside over an open flame. Here we are making a baked paella in the oven for convenience. You can vary the vegetables to your tastes. You can also change up the vegetables in this dish seasonally for more options.

2 tablespoons extra-virgin olive oil

1 medium onion, sliced

1 red or green bell pepper, seeded and sliced

3 cloves of garlic, chopped

¼ cup dry white wine

1 cup Arborio rice

3 cups Vegetable Broth (page 112), divided

1 cup canned or cooked chickpeas, drained and rinsed

1 teaspoon smoked paprika

1 cup green beans

1 cup broccoli florets

½ cup frozen peas

1. Preheat the oven to 350°F.

2. In a large ovenproof skillet or braising pan, heat the olive oil over medium heat. Add the onion, bell pepper, and garlic and cook for about 10 minutes until the vegetables are softened. Transfer the veggies to a plate.

3. Pour the wine into the skillet and deglaze, stirring to scrape up any browned bits on the bottom. Add the rice and mix with the wine until coated.

4. Add 1 cup of broth and the paprika. Stir, and cook for 5 minutes.

5. Add the chickpeas and 1 cup of broth, and stir again. Return the vegetables to the skillet, along with the green beans, broccoli, and peas on top of the rice. Push them down into the rice and chickpea mixture, but do not stir. Add the remaining cup of broth and bring to a boil.

6. Cover the skillet, transfer to the oven, and bake for 40 minutes.

7. Uncover the skillet and peek at the dish. If it looks dry, add ⅓ cup of water to the skillet. Return to the oven and bake for another 10 minutes, uncovered.

FLEX TIP: Place 1 pound of raw mussels in their shells studded into the rice in the last 10 minutes of cooking for a seafood option. For a meat option, include 1 sliced hot Italian pork sausage in the first step when you are sautéing the vegetables.

PER SERVING: Calories: 353; Fat: 8g; Protein: 10g; Carbohydrates: 60g, Fiber: 8g; Sugar: 7g; Sodium: 119mg

Baked Falafel Bowl

QUICK PREP.

SERVES: 4 | **PREP TIME:** 5 MINUTES | **COOK TIME:** 40 MINUTES

Falafels are chickpea patties usually deep-fried, but here we are baking them for a healthier option. Be sure to use dried chickpeas, not canned, to get the proper texture. Create a bowl with a chopped salad, hummus, and a few olives, and you have a healthy Mediterranean-inspired meal.

FOR THE FALAFEL

3 tablespoons extra-virgin olive oil, divided

1 cup dried chickpeas

1 medium onion, rough chopped

2 cloves of garlic, peeled

3 tablespoons chopped flat-leaf parsley, stems removed

1 tablespoon all-purpose flour

1 teaspoon ground coriander

1 teaspoon ground cumin

1 teaspoon salt

⅛ teaspoon cayenne pepper

2 cups Hummus (page 116)

20 Kalamata olives, pitted

FOR THE CHOPPED SALAD

1 cup diced tomatoes

1 cucumber, peeled and diced

¼ cup red onion, diced

2 tablespoons freshly squeezed lemon juice

¼ cup extra-virgin olive oil

½ teaspoon dried oregano

Pinch salt

TO MAKE THE FALAFEL

1. Preheat the oven to 350°F. Line a rimmed baking sheet with parchment paper and lightly brush with olive oil.

2. Put the chickpeas in a large saucepan and cover with water by 1 inch. Bring to a boil over high heat, reduce the heat to low, and simmer for 15 minutes. Drain the chickpeas and let them cool.

3. In a food processor or blender, combine the onion, garlic, parsley, flour, 1 tablespoon of olive oil, coriander, cumin, salt, and cayenne. Pulse a few times to combine. Add the chickpeas and process to form a thick paste.

4. Scoop out about 1 tablespoon of the falafel mixture, roll it in your hands to create a ball, then flatten into a patty about 2 inches wide. You should get 12 to 15 patties.

5. Place the patties on the baking sheet, brush them with the remaining 2 tablespoons of olive oil, and bake for 15 minutes. Flip and bake for 10 more minutes, or until lightly browned.

TO MAKE THE SALAD

6. In a medium bowl, combine the tomatoes, cucumber, red onion, lemon juice, olive oil, oregano, and salt, and toss to combine.

7. Divide salad equally among four serving bowls. Top each with ½ cup of hummus, 5 Kalamata olives, and 3 to 4 falafel patties.

FLEX TIP: For a creamy option, top each bowl with a dollop of tzatziki sauce made with Greek yogurt, olive oil, cucumbers, garlic, and dill.

PER SERVING: Calories: 684; Fat: 40g; Protein: 18g; Carbohydrates: 68g, Fiber: 13g; Sugar: 10g; Sodium: 1148mg

Super-Seed Chocolate Bark ◆ 102

CHAPTER 7

Desserts

Super-Seed Chocolate Bark ◆ 102

Peanut Butter Granola Bars ◆ 103

Mango Plantain N'Ice Cream ◆ 104

Chocolate-Peppermint N'Ice Cream ◆ 105

Chocolate Covered Frozen Banana Nuggets with Nuts ◆ 106

Apple and Pear Cake ◆ 107

Seasonal Fruit Galette ◆ 108

Oatmeal Hazelnut Raisin Cookies ◆ 109

Super-Seed Chocolate Bark

5/FEWER ING. FAST FAV.

SERVES: 6 TO 8 | **PREP TIME:** 10 MINUTES | **COOK TIME:** 20 MINUTES

Yes, chocolate can be plant-based! Look for cacao percentages between 55 and 85 percent and read the label to avoid milk-derived ingredients such as casein, milk fat or solids, and whey. Add whatever nuts and seeds you have on hand to the simple melted-chocolate base.

1 cup vegan dark chocolate chips, chunks, or chopped bars

¼ cup chopped unsalted pistachios

1 tablespoon sesame seeds

1 tablespoon raw hulled pumpkin seeds

1. Line a baking sheet with parchment paper.

2. Fill the bottom of a double boiler or a medium saucepan with a few inches of water and bring to a boil over high heat. Lower the heat to medium to keep the water at a simmer. Place the chocolate in the top of the double boiler or in a heatproof bowl that fits over the saucepan (the bottom of the bowl should not touch the water). Using a silicone spatula, stir frequently until the chocolate has melted. Remove from the heat.

3. In a small bowl, combine the pistachios, sesame seeds, and pumpkin seeds.

4. Scrape the melted chocolate into the center of the baking sheet and spread it into a layer about ¼-inch thick (the chocolate won't cover the entire pan). Sprinkle the nuts and seeds over the top. Refrigerate for at least 1 hour before serving.

5. Break the chocolate bark into 10 to 12 rough pieces. Serve immediately or store in an airtight container at room temperature for up to a week or in the refrigerator for up to 2 weeks.

TIP: This is candy, so eat up! You can also crumble it over a fruity yogurt parfait or try adding ¼ cup crumbled bark to your favorite cookie recipe.

PER SERVING (1 PIECE): Calories: 183; Fat: 12g; Protein: 3g; Carbohydrates: 18g; Fiber: 2g; Sugar: 5g; Sodium: 9mg

Peanut Butter Granola Bars

5/FEWER ING. **FAST FAV.**

MAKES: 12 BARS | **PREP TIME:** 10 MINUTES, PLUS 20 MINUTES TO CHILL

Most processed granola bars are high in sugar, fat, and sodium and include many chemicals for shelf stability. Making your own granola bars ensures fresh, quality ingredients and allows you to customize them.

---

1 cup packed pitted dates

¼ cup pure maple syrup

¼ cup creamy natural peanut butter or almond butter

1 cup coarsely chopped roasted, unsalted almonds

1½ cups old-fashioned oats

1. In a food processor, combine the dates, maple syrup, and peanut butter. Process for 1 to 2 minutes, or until the mixture comes together and feels slightly sticky. Stop right before or as it starts to turn into a ball of loose dough.

2. Add the almonds and oats and process for 1 minute. Press the dough into an 8-inch-square baking dish and cover with plastic wrap. Refrigerate for 20 minutes.

3. Cut the chilled mixture into 12 bars and refrigerate in a sealable bag or airtight container for 1 to 2 weeks or freeze for up to 6 months.

> **TIP:** If adding more nuts, seeds, or dried fruit, keep the total addition to under 1 cup, so the bars retain their shape once cut. Transfer the dough mixture to a bowl and use a heavy wooden spoon to incorporate the add-ins. If adding seeds, I suggest sunflower, hemp, or pumpkin; stir them in last and use up to ¼ cup total. Toast your oats in a 350°F oven for 10 minutes to add even more flavor.

PER SERVING (1 BAR): Calories: 181; Fat: 9g; Protein: 5g; Carbohydrates: 24g, Fiber: 4g; Sugar: 12g; Sodium: 2mg

Mango Plantain N'Ice Cream

ONE-POT   QUICK PREP.

SERVES: 4 | **PREP TIME:** 5 MINUTES, PLUS OVERNIGHT TO CHILL

If you haven't heard of "n'ice cream," you're in for a treat. This plant-based take on ice cream will satisfy your sweet tooth without the high sugar and fat content. Most recipes use frozen bananas, but here we're replacing them with ripe plantains, which result in a different flavor profile and texture that complement the mango quite nicely.

2 plantains, peeled, cut into slices, and frozen

1 cup frozen mango pieces

½ cup unsweetened nondairy milk, plus more as needed

2 pitted dates or 1 tablespoon pure maple syrup

1 teaspoon vanilla extract

Juice of 1 lime

1. In a high-speed blender or food processor, combine the frozen plantains, mango, milk, dates, vanilla, and lime juice. Blend for 30 seconds. Scrape down the sides and blend again until smooth, scraping down the sides again if the mixture doesn't look smooth. Add more milk, 1 tablespoon at a time, as needed.

2. Refrigerate leftovers in an airtight container for a smoothie-like consistency or freeze for a firm ice cream texture. If frozen, thaw slightly before serving.

TIP: The best ripeness for this recipe is when the plantain skin is mostly black with a little yellow showing. The plantain should still be firm to the touch but have some give, like a ripe peach. To prepare ahead of this recipe, cut your peeled plantains into ¼-inch-thick coins and freeze them on a parchment paper–lined baking sheet, then transfer them to a freezer bag.

PER SERVING (1 CUP): Calories: 208; Fat: 1g; Protein: 2g; Carbohydrates: 52g, Fiber: 3g; Sugar: 20g; Sodium: 24mg

Chocolate-Peppermint N'Ice Cream

5/FEWER ING. | **FAST FAV.** | **QUICK PREP.**

SERVES: 2 | **PREP TIME:** 5 MINUTES

Keeping some bananas ready to go in your freezer is always a good idea. A helpful tip for n'ice cream is making sure that the bananas are well-ripened before peeling and freezing. Chocolate and peppermint are a perfect combination for an after-dinner treat or midday snack on a warm summer day.

3 frozen ripe bananas, broken into thirds

3 tablespoons plant-based milk

2 tablespoons cocoa powder

⅛ teaspoon peppermint extract

1. In a food processor, combine the bananas, milk, cocoa powder, and peppermint.

2. Process on medium speed for 30 to 60 seconds, or until the bananas have been blended into smooth, soft-serve consistency and serve. (If you notice any banana pieces stuck toward the top and sides of the food processor, you may need to stop and scrape them down with a spatula, then pulse until smooth.)

TIP: If you don't have a food processor, a blender works, too. For a high-speed blender, use the tamper tool to ensure all the banana gets blended properly. For a less powerful blender, use ¼ to ½ cup plant-based milk instead of 3 tablespoons.

PER SERVING: Calories: 173; Fat: 2g; Protein: 3g; Carbohydrates: 43g; Fiber: 6g; Sugar: 22g; Sodium: 11mg

Chocolate Covered Frozen Banana Nuggets with Nuts

5/FEWER ING. **QUICK PREP.**

SERVES: 4 TO 6 | **PREP TIME**: 5 MINUTES, PLUS 30 MINUTES TO CHILL

Kids love these fun frozen treats. They are easy enough for them to help make as well. Not only are they tasty, but these frozen bananas are also a good source of potassium and antioxidants. They keep in the freezer for up to a week.

12 ounces vegan dark chocolate

4 bananas, cut into 2-inch pieces

½ cup chopped peanuts (or any nut of your choice)

1. Line a baking sheet with wax paper or parchment paper.

2. Over a double boiler, melt the chocolate until smooth, being careful not to let it boil. Alternatively, you could melt the chocolate in a glass bowl in a microwave oven at 30-second increments.

3. With a fork or slotted spoon, dip each piece of banana in melted chocolate to completely coat. Allow excess chocolate to drip off before placing it on the baking sheet. Sprinkle immediately with chopped nuts. Repeat with all the banana pieces.

4. Place the tray in the freezer for at least 30 minutes before serving.

FLEX TIP: These also make a fun topping for sundaes. If you're not watching your dairy intake, you could also make these with milk chocolate.

PER SERVING: Calories: 716; Fat: 46g; Protein: 13g; Carbohydrates: 69g; Fiber: 14g; Sugar: 36g; Sodium: 20mg

Apple and Pear Cake

QUICK PREP.

SERVES: 4 TO 6 | **PREP TIME:** 5 MINUTES | **COOK TIME:** 60 MINUTES

This classic Italian cake gets its sweetness from fruit instead of added sugar. Not only does it make a tasty and healthier dessert, but it also works as a quick breakfast or midday snack.

1 cup all-purpose flour

2½ teaspoons cream of tartar

Pinch salt

Zest of ½ lemon

¼ cup vegetable oil

¼ cup plant-based milk

3 tablespoons maple syrup

2 apples, peeled, cored, and diced

2 pears, peeled, cored, and diced

¼ cup slivered almonds

1. Preheat the oven to 350°F. Line a 9-inch round cake pan with parchment paper.

2. Sift together in a bowl the flour, cream of tartar, and salt. Add the lemon zest.

3. In a separate bowl, whisk together the vegetable oil, milk, and maple syrup, and stir into the dry ingredients. If the batter seems dry, you can add a little more milk.

4. Fold the apples, pears, and almonds into the batter, and transfer the mixture to the cake pan.

5. Bake in the oven for 1 hour or until a toothpick inserted into the center comes out clean.

FLEX TIP: This cake goes very well with a scoop of vanilla ice cream (or n'ice cream) and a dollop of whipped cream.

PER SERVING: Calories: 401; Fat: 18g; Protein: 5g; Carbohydrates: 58g; Fiber: 6g; Sugar: 24g; Sodium: 52mg

Seasonal Fruit Galette

SERVES: 8 | **PREP TIME:** 15 MINUTES | **COOK TIME:** 45 MINUTES

Have fun with your galette and experiment with different fruits depending on what is in season. Apples and pears work well in autumn and winter. Peaches work well in spring and summer.

1 store-bought or homemade vegan pie crust
5 apples, peeled, cored, and sliced
½ cup all-purpose flour
⅓ cup granulated sugar
1 tablespoon freshly squeezed lemon juice
1 teaspoon salt
1 tablespoon coarse sugar, like turbinado or demerara (optional)

1. Preheat the oven to 400°F. Place the pie crust into a 9-inch pie pan.

2. In a large bowl, toss the apples, flour, sugar, lemon juice, and salt.

3. Pour the apple mixture into the pie pan and fold the sides of the crust over the apple filling, overlapping them with pleats but leaving the center of the pie uncovered.

4. Bake for 40 to 45 minutes, sprinkling the top with sugar halfway through (if using) until the crust is golden brown.

5. Let cool before slicing.

> **FLEX TIP:** Use a standard pie crust made with butter. If you don't have a pie pan, this also works on a baking sheet. The pie is not too wet, so it maintains its shape on the sheet.

PER SERVING: Calories: 214; Fat: 6g; Protein: 2g; Carbohydrates: 39g, Fiber: 2g; Sugar: 21g; Sodium: 379mg

Oatmeal Hazelnut Raisin Cookies

(FAST FAV.)

MAKES: 2 DOZEN | **PREP TIME:** 15 MINUTES | **COOK TIME:** 10 MINUTES

1 tablespoon ground flaxseed plus 3 tablespoons water
¾ cup all-purpose flour
½ teaspoon baking soda
½ teaspoon cinnamon

¼ teaspoon salt
7 tablespoons vegan butter, at room temperature
¼ cup granulated sugar
⅓ cup packed light brown sugar

½ teaspoon vanilla extract
1½ cups old-fashioned oats
¼ cup raisins
¼ cup chopped hazelnuts

1. Preheat the oven to 350°F. Line a baking sheet with parchment paper.

2. Mix the flaxseed and water in a small bowl and put it in the refrigerator for 10 minutes.

3. In a medium bowl, combine the flour, baking soda, cinnamon, and salt.

4. In a large bowl, beat the butter, sugar, and brown sugar with an electric mixer until ingredients are light and fluffy, about 4 minutes.

5. Add the flaxseed egg and vanilla to the creamed mixture and beat until combined. Add the flour mixture and beat until a soft dough forms.

6. Fold the oats, raisins, and hazelnuts into the dough by hand until well combined.

7. Working in batches, drop the cookie dough by tablespoons onto the baking sheet, leaving a little room for them to spread. You should be able to fit about 15 cookies per sheet.

8. Bake for 8 to 10 minutes, until golden brown. Allow the cookies to cool for 1 minute on the baking sheet, then transfer to a wire cooling rack.

9. Repeat with the remaining cookie dough. This recipe will make about 2 dozen cookies.

FLEX TIP: Swap the flaxseed and water for 1 egg and butter for the vegan butter.

PER SERVING (1 COOKIE): Calories: 106; Fat: 5g; Protein: 2g; Carbohydrates: 14g, Fiber: 1g; Sugar: 6g; Sodium: 53mg

Roasted Jalapeño and Lime Guacamole ◆ 114

CHAPTER 8

Sauces and Staples

Vegetable Broth ◆ 112

Plant Pesto ◆ 113

Roasted Jalapeño and Lime Guacamole ◆ 114

Basic Tomato Basil Sauce ◆ 115

Hummus ◆ 116

Vegan Béchamel ◆ 117

Spicy Peanut Sauce ◆ 118

Romesco Sauce ◆ 119

Vegetable Broth

ONE-POT

MAKES: 8 CUPS | **PREP TIME:** 10 MINUTES | **COOK TIME:** 40 MINUTES

Vegetable broth is very versatile and is used frequently in the recipes in this book. Make a batch on the weekend and use it throughout the week. It is excellent as a base ingredient or to add moisture to meals. You can easily buy this in the supermarket, but nothing beats homemade. This broth also freezes well.

8 cups water

4 large carrots, coarsely chopped

4 celery ribs, coarsely chopped

2 large onions, coarsely chopped

1 cup sliced mushrooms

4 or 6 cloves of garlic unpeeled, halved

2 bay leaves

1 teaspoon dried basil

1 teaspoon dried oregano

1 teaspoon dried parsley

1 teaspoon garlic powder

1 teaspoon salt (optional)

1 teaspoon freshly ground black pepper

1. In a large stockpot, combine the water, carrots, celery, onions, mushrooms, garlic, bay leaves, basil, oregano, parsley, garlic powder, salt (if using), and pepper. Bring to a low boil over high heat. Reduce the heat to low and simmer for 40 minutes.

2. Strain the broth through a fine-mesh strainer or cheesecloth and discard the solids.

3. The broth can be refrigerated in an airtight container for up to 1 week or frozen for up to 3 months.

> **TIP:** When meal prepping or reheating prepped meals later in the week, set the jar of broth on the counter and add some whenever you need a little liquid for reheating or a splash of flavor.

PER SERVING (1 CUP): Calories: 15; Fat: 0g; Protein: 0g; Carbohydrates: 3g; Fiber: 1g; Sugar: 1g; Sodium: 86mg

Plant Pesto

5/FEWER ING. | **FAST FAV.** | **ONE-POT**

MAKES: 1½ CUPS | **PREP TIME:** 10 MINUTES

Basil and pine nuts are traditional ingredients in pesto. Here we're using kale and pistachios for a pop of flavor and a nutrition boost. The coarse kale gives the verdant pesto an unexpected texture, and the pistachios lend a protein punch.

2 cups tightly packed chopped, stemmed kale leaves

½ cup shelled unsalted pistachios

3 cloves of garlic, coarsely chopped

¼ cup nutritional yeast or vegan Parmesan

¼ cup freshly squeezed lemon juice

1 teaspoon salt

1 to 2 tablespoons extra-virgin olive oil (optional)

1. In a food processor or blender, combine the kale, pistachios, and garlic, and pulse until the nuts are ground into small bits.

2. While pulsing, add the nutritional yeast, lemon juice, and salt. With the motor running, slowly drizzle in the olive oil (if using), and process until a thick paste forms.

3. Use immediately or refrigerate for up to 5 days.

TIP: If you skip the oil here, you'll want to drizzle in a bit of water for texture, so the pesto is less thick.

PER SERVING (¼ CUP): Calories: 95; Fat: 5g; Protein: 5g; Carbohydrates: 8g, Fiber: 3g; Sugar: 1g; Sodium: 558mg

Roasted Jalapeño and Lime Guacamole

5/FEWER ING. | **FAST FAV.** | **QUICK PREP.**

SERVES: 4 | **PREP TIME:** 5 MINUTES | **COOK TIME:** 10 MINUTES

This guacamole brings heat and a touch of sweetness from the roasted jalapeño, a pop of sourness from the lime, and the wonderful creamy texture and unique flavor of a ripe avocado.

2 or 3 jalapeño peppers
  (depending on your
  preferred level of heat)

1 avocado, peeled and pitted

1 tablespoon freshly
  squeezed lime juice

1. Preheat the oven to 400°F. Line a baking sheet with parchment paper.

2. Place the jalapeños on the baking sheet and roast for 8 minutes.

3. Slice the jalapeños down the center and remove the seeds. Then cut the top stem off and dice them into ⅛-inch pieces. Wash your hands immediately after handling the jalapeños.

4. In a medium bowl, use a fork to mash together the avocado, jalapeño, and lime juice. Continue mashing and mixing until the guacamole reaches your preferred consistency and serve.

> **TIP:** A fun way to change up the guacamole or lessen the amount of fat per serving is to blend 1 cup of steamed sweet peas into a smooth puree, then mix the peas in with the guacamole for spicy-sweet pea guacamole.

PER SERVING: Calories: 77; Fat: 7g; Protein: 1g; Carbohydrates: 5g, Fiber: 3g; Sugar: 2g; Sodium: 5mg

Basic Tomato Basil Sauce

5/FEWER ING. | **FAST FAV.** | **ONE-POT**

MAKES: 4 CUPS | **PREP TIME:** 10 MINUTES | **COOK TIME:** 20 MINUTES

It's always a good idea to have a basic tomato sauce recipe in your repertoire. You can use it as a pasta sauce, on sandwiches, or to add flavor to soups and stews. It's used in a few recipes throughout this book.

¼ cup extra-virgin olive oil
4 cloves of garlic crushed
1 (28-ounce) can crushed
  tomatoes

1 cup water
⅛ teaspoon salt
⅛ teaspoon freshly ground
  black pepper

1 cup chopped fresh basil

1. In a medium saucepan over medium heat, heat the olive oil.

2. Add the garlic and cook for 1 minute until fragrant.

3. Stir in the tomatoes, water, salt, and pepper. Bring to a boil, cover the pan, and simmer for 15 minutes, stirring occasionally.

4. Stir in the basil and cook for 2 to 3 minutes more. Refrigerate the cooled leftovers in an airtight container for up to 1 week, or freeze for up to 6 weeks.

PER SERVING (½ CUP): Calories: 88; Fat: 7g; Protein: 1g; Carbohydrates: 8g, Fiber: 2g; Sugar: 3g; Sodium: 165mg

Hummus

5/FEWER ING. | FAST FAV. | ONE-POT

SERVES: 4 | **PREP TIME:** 20 MINUTES

Hummus is a chickpea dip traditionally made with garlic and tahini. You can also add vegetables, hot peppers, olives, or various spices to make flavorful variations. Use it as a dip, a sandwich spread, or a condiment.

---

1 (15-ounce) can chickpeas, drained and rinsed
½ cup plus 3 tablespoons cold water, divided

4 cloves of garlic peeled
½ cup freshly squeezed lemon juice
¼ cup tahini

½ teaspoon ground cumin
Salt

1. In a food processor or blender, combine the chickpeas, ½ cup of cold water, and garlic. Process for about 5 minutes or until well combined.

2. Add the lemon juice, tahini, and cumin, and season with salt. Process into a smooth, spreadable paste, about 2 minutes more. If your hummus is a little thick, add more cold water, 1 tablespoon at a time, and process until it reaches the desired consistency.

3. Taste the hummus and season with more salt, as needed.

> **TIP:** For a sweet variation, try making sweet potato hummus. You will need 2 sweet potatoes, 1 tablespoon peeled, grated fresh ginger, 2 peeled cloves of garlic, ¼ cup freshly squeezed lemon juice, grated zest of 1 lemon, ¼ cup tahini, ¼ teaspoon ground cumin, and ⅛ teaspoon salt. Peel and wrap the potatoes, ginger, and garlic in aluminum foil. Place the packet on a baking sheet and bake in a 400°F oven for 1 hour. Remove from the oven, mash or process together, and stir in the lemon juice, lemon zest, tahini, cumin, and salt.

PER SERVING: Calories: 203; Fat: 10g; Protein: 8g; Carbohydrates: 22g; Fiber: 6g; Sugar: 4g; Sodium: 67mg

Vegan Béchamel

5/FEWER ING. FAST FAV. ONE-POT

MAKES: 2½ CUPS | **PREP TIME:** 10 MINUTES | **COOK TIME:** 10 MINUTES

This French sauce is sometimes used as an ingredient to thicken other sauces. In northern Italy, béchamel is often used in lasagna Bolognese in place of ricotta cheese. Make this quick sauce when you are ready to use it. It does not like to wait around.

¼ cup vegan butter or margarine

⅓ cup all-purpose flour

2 cups nondairy milk

½ teaspoon salt

¼ teaspoon freshly ground black pepper

Pinch nutmeg

1. In a medium saucepan, melt the butter over medium heat. Add the flour a little at a time, and whisk until it forms a roux, or a paste. Be careful not to let the mixture brown.

2. Add the milk a little at a time, continuously whisking each addition until smooth.

3. Reduce the heat to low. Add salt, pepper, and nutmeg. Simmer gently until the sauce thickens, stirring frequently, for about 10 minutes.

4. Use immediately.

FLEX TIP: Traditional béchamel is made with unsalted butter and whole cow's milk.

PER SERVING (¼ CUP): Calories: 72; Fat: 5g; Protein: 2g; Carbohydrates: 4g, Fiber: 0g; Sugar: 0g; Sodium: 135mg

Spicy Peanut Sauce

FAST FAV. ONE-POT QUICK PREP.

MAKES: 2 CUPS | **PREP TIME:** 5 MINUTES | **COOK TIME:** 10 MINUTES

This recipe is my Mediterranean-inspired version of the spicy peanut sauce you get in Thai restaurants. The heat comes from the Calabrian chili paste and red pepper flakes. This sauce goes very nicely with vegetables and chicken. You can serve this sauce hot or cold.

1 cup unsweetened vanilla almond milk

½ cup all-natural peanut butter

1 teaspoon honey or maple syrup

1 teaspoon Calabrian chili paste

1 clove of garlic, minced

¼ teaspoon freshly ground black pepper

¼ teaspoon red pepper flakes

Juice from ½ lime

2 tablespoons water (if needed)

1. In a small saucepan over medium heat, add the almond milk, peanut butter, honey, chili paste, garlic, pepper, and red pepper flakes, and stir to combine. Bring to a boil.

2. Reduce the heat, and simmer for 5 minutes until it thickens.

3. Remove from heat and stir in the lime juice. This sauce may thicken quite a bit. You can add a little water to thin it out.

4. Allow to cool or serve hot.

> **TIP:** To make a traditional Thai peanut sauce, substitute coconut milk for the almond milk and Thai chili paste for the Calabrian.

PER SERVING (2 TABLESPOONS): Calories: 55; Fat: 5g; Protein: 2g; Carbohydrates: 3g; Fiber: 1g; Sugar: 1g; Sodium: 15mg

Romesco Sauce

FAST FAV. | ONE-POT

MAKES: 1½ CUPS | **PREP TIME**: 10 MINUTES

Romesco sauce is made of roasted red bell peppers, tomatoes, and almonds. It comes from the Catalonia region of Spain and is traditionally served with fish, but this spicy sauce can be used in many ways. It makes a unique sandwich spread or a tasty accompaniment to many dishes.

1 cup chopped roasted red bell pepper

½ cup toasted almonds

2 tablespoons tomato paste

1 tablespoon sherry vinegar

1 clove of garlic

1 teaspoon smoked paprika

½ teaspoon salt

½ teaspoon cayenne pepper (or to taste)

½ teaspoon freshly ground black pepper

½ cup extra-virgin olive oil

1. In a food processor or blender, combine the roasted pepper, almonds, tomato paste, vinegar, garlic, paprika, salt, cayenne, and black pepper, and pulse until finely chopped.

2. Scrape down the sides. With the food processor running, slowly drizzle in the olive oil until smooth.

TIP: If you want this sauce to be thicker, add bread crumbs a little at a time. This is the traditional method for thickening this Spanish sauce.

PER SERVING (2 TABLESPOONS): Calories: 121; Fat: 12g; Protein: 2g; Carbohydrates: 3g; Fiber: 1g; Sugar: 1g; Sodium: 99mg

MEASUREMENT CONVERSIONS

VOLUME EQUIVALENTS	US STANDARD	US STANDARD (OUNCES)	METRIC (APPROXIMATE)
LIQUID	2 tablespoons	1 fl. oz.	30 mL
	¼ cup	2 fl. oz.	60 mL
	½ cup	4 fl. oz.	120 mL
	1 cup	8 fl. oz.	240 mL
	1½ cups	12 fl. oz.	355 mL
	2 cups or 1 pint	16 fl. oz.	475 mL
	4 cups or 1 quart	32 fl. oz.	1 L
	1 gallon	128 fl. oz.	4 L
DRY	⅛ teaspoon		0.5 mL
	¼ teaspoon		1 mL
	½ teaspoon		2 mL
	¾ teaspoon		4 mL
	1 teaspoon		5 mL
	1 tablespoon		15 mL
	¼ cup		59 mL
	⅓ cup		79 mL
	½ cup		118 mL
	⅔ cup		156 mL
	¾ cup		177 mL
	1 cup		235 mL
	2 cups or 1 pint		475 mL
	3 cups		700 mL
	4 cups or 1 quart		1 L
	½ gallon		2 L
	1 gallon		4 L

OVEN TEMPERATURES

FAHRENHEIT	CELSIUS (APPROXIMATE)
250°F	120°C
300°F	150°C
325°F	165°C
350°F	180°C
375°F	190°C
400°F	200°C
425°F	220°C
450°F	230°C

WEIGHT EQUIVALENTS

US STANDARD	METRIC (APPROXIMATE)
½ ounce	15 g
1 ounce	30 g
2 ounces	60 g
4 ounces	115 g
8 ounces	225 g
12 ounces	340 g
16 ounces or 1 pound	455 g

REFERENCES

American Heart Association. "How Does Plant-Forward (Plant-Based) Eating Benefit Your Health?" Accessed November 5, 2021. Heart.org/en/healthy-living/healthy-eating/eat-smart/nutrition-basics/how-does-plant-forward-eating-benefit-your-health.

Cornell University. "U.S. Could Feed 800 Million People with Grain That Livestock Eat, Cornell Ecologist Advises Animal Scientists." Published August 7, 1997. News.Cornell.edu/stories/1997/08/us-could-feed-800-million-people-grain-livestock-eat.

Ferdowsian, Hope, and Neal D. Bardnard. "Effects of Plant-Based Diets on Plasma Lipids." *American Journal of Cardiology*, October 1, 2009. https://www.ajconline.org/article/S0002-9149(09)01099-6/fulltext.

Jiang, Xian et al. "Increased Consumption of Fruit and Vegetables Is Related to a Reduced Risk of Cognitive Impairment and Dementia: Meta-Analysis." *Frontiers in Aging Neuroscience*. Accessed November 5, 2021. NCBI.NLM.NIH.gov/pmc/articles/PMC5293796.

Kim, Hyunju et al. "Healthy Plant-Based Diets Are Associated with Lower Risk of All-Cause Mortality in US Adults." *Journal of Nutrition*. Accessed November 5, 2021. PubMed.NCBI.NLM.NIH.gov/29659968.

Kim, Hyunju et al. "Plant-Based Diets Are Associated With a Lower Risk of Incident Cardiovascular Disease, Cardiovascular Disease Mortality, and All-Cause Mortality in a General Population of Middle-Aged Adults." *Journal of the American Heart Association*. Published August 7, 2019. AHAJournals.org/doi/10.1161/JAHA.119.012865.

Malar, D. Sheeja, and K. Pandima Devi. "Dietary Polyphenols for Treatment of Alzheimer's Disease—Future Research and Development." *Current Pharmaceutical Biotechnology*. Accessed November 5, 2021. PubMed.NCBI.NLM.NIH.gov/25312617.

Mayo Clinic. "How Plant-Based Food Helps Fight Cancer." Accessed November 5, 2021. MayoClinic.org/healthy-lifestyle/nutrition-and-healthy-eating/in-depth/how-plant-based-food-helps-fight-cancer/art-20457590.

Mayo Clinic. "Nuts and Your Heart: Eating Nuts for Heart Health." Accessed November 5, 2021. MayoClinic.org/diseases-conditions/heart-disease/in-depth/nuts/art-20046635.

Mayo Clinic, "Whole Grains: Hearty Options for a Healthy Diet." Accessed November 5, 2021. MayoClinic.org/healthy-lifestyle/nutrition-and-healthy-eating/in-depth/whole-grains/art-20047826.

Satija, Ambika et al. "Healthful and Unhealthful Plant-Based Diets and the Risk of Coronary Heart Disease in U.S. Adults." *Journal of the American College of Cardiology*. Accessed November 5, 2021. JACC.org/doi/10.1016/j.jacc.2017.05.047.

Satija, Ambika et al. "Plant-Based Dietary Patterns and Incidence of Type 2 Diabetes in US Men and Women: Results from Three Prospective Cohort Studies." *PLoS Medicine*. Published June 14, 2016. PubMed.NCBI.NLM.NIH.gov/27299701.

Springmann, Marco et al. "Options for Keeping the Food System within Environmental Limits." *Nature*. Published October 10, 2018. Nature.com/articles/s41586-018-0594-0.

University of Chester. "Antioxidants in Fresh and Frozen Fruit and Vegetables: Impact Study of Varying Storage Conditions." Accessed November 5, 2021. BFFF.co.uk/wp-content/uploads/2013/09/Leatherhead-Chester-Antioxidant-Reports-2013.pdf.

Yokoyama, Yoko et al. "Vegetarian Diets and Blood Pressure: A Meta-analysis." *JAMA Internal Medicine*. Accessed November 5, 2021. PubMed.NCBI.NLM.NIH.gov/24566947.

INDEX

A

almond butter, 31, 103
almonds, whole, 7, 15, 17, 18, 20
apples, 8, 11
  Apple and Pear Cake, 107
  Seasonal Fruit Galette, 108
applesauce, unsweetened, 17, 26, 27
asparagus, 8
  Asparagus and Leek Soup, 69
  Skillet Asparagus with Lemon Zest, 41
avocado, 8, 9, 15, 18, 70
  Chopped Avocado Chickpea
    Salad with Olives, 53
  Green Shakshuka, 34
  Roasted Jalapeño and Lime
    Guacamole, 114

B

baking powder, 17, 20, 26, 27, 28
banana, 15, 18
  Chocolate Covered Frozen Banana
    Nuggets with Nuts, 106
  Chocolate-Peppermint N'Ice Cream, 105
  Smoothie Bowls, 3 Ways, 31
basil (dried), 16, 19, 29, 45, 66, 112
basil, fresh, 15, 18, 55, 78, 84, 91, 92
  Basic Tomato Basil Sauce, 115
bay leaf, 16, 112
beans, 7
  black beans, 7, 17, 20, 63, 82
  butter beans, 17, 59

cannellini, 7, 11, 20
  pinto, 7, 11, 17, 63
berries
  blueberries, 8
  mixed/assorted, 1, 16, 18
  Smoothie Bowls, 3 Ways, 31
  strawberries, 8, 31
black pepper, 16, 19
bok choy, 8, 18, 70
bread
  bread crumbs, 17, 66, 83, 119
  French, 45, 55, 76
  fresh, freezing, 12
  pita, 20, 53, 62
  rye, 9, 59
  sourdough, 20, 29, 33
  whole wheat, 9, 83
bread crumbs, 17, 66, 83, 119
Breakfast
  Carrot Cake Oatmeal, 25
  GLT Sandwich, 33
  Green Shakshuka, 34
  Mushroom and Scallion
    Chickpea Omelet, 28
  Oatmeal-Raisin Breakfast Bowl, 24
  Pear and Farro Bowl, 30
  Polenta with Potato and Red Onion, 32
  Smoothie Bowl, 3 Ways, 31
  Veggie and White Bean Scramble, 29
  Whole Wheat Pancakes, 26
  Zucchini-Carrot Oatmeal Muffins, 27
broccoli, 8, 19, 93

broccoli rabe, 8
  Broccoli Rabe with Red Pepper Flakes, 40
broth
  Vegetable Broth, 112

C

cabbage
  green, 8, 15, 47, 63, 86
  red, 19, 70
cancer prevention, 4
capers, 20, 54, 60, 91
carrots, 15, 19, 27, 42, 66, 68,
    71, 72, 75, 86, 112
cayenne pepper, 19, 43, 48, 56, 98, 119
celery, 15, 19, 56, 68, 71, 72, 75, 87, 112
cheese
  Italian blend, 19, 88
  mozzarella, vegan style, 16, 57
  parmesan, 19, 32, 34, 39, 45,
    52, 62, 84, 93, 113
chicken
  breasts, boneless/skinless,
    16, 40, 43, 63, 85
  broth, 75, 77
  ground, 16, 66, 75
  thighs, boneless/skinless, 90
chickpeas, 7, 17, 20, 52, 60, 96, 98
  Baked Falafel Bowl, 98
  chickpea flour, 17
  Chopped Avocado Chickpea
    Salad with Olives, 53
  Hearty Chickpea Burgers, 83
  Hummus, 116
  Minestrone with Beans, 71

  Mushroom and Scallion
    Chickpea Omelet, 28
chili paste, Calabrian, 17, 118
chili powder, 16, 19, 82, 83
chipotle powder, 67
chocolate
  Chocolate Covered Frozen Banana
    Nuggets with Nuts, 106
  Chocolate-Peppermint N'Ice Cream, 105
  Super-Seed Chocolate Bark, 102
cilantro, 15, 47, 63
cinnamon, 16, 19, 24, 25, 26, 30, 60, 109
coconut flakes, 17, 20, 31
coconut water, 20, 31
condiments, 11
coriander, 98
cornstarch, 17, 85
cumin, ground, 16, 19, 56, 60, 74, 85, 98, 116
curry paste
  Red Thai, 17, 20, 70, 85

D

dates, pitted, 20, 24, 103, 104
Desserts
  Apple and Pear Cake, 107
  Chocolate Covered Frozen Banana
    Nuggets with Nuts, 106
  Chocolate-Peppermint N'Ice Cream, 105
  Mango Plantain N'Ice Cream, 104
  Oatmeal Hazelnut Raisin Cookies, 109
  Peanut Butter Granola Bars, 103
  Seasonal Fruit Galette, 108
  Super-Seed Chocolate Bark, 102
diabetes, 4

E

eggplant, 15, 45
  Smoky Eggplant and Yellow
    Squash Soup, 74
eggs, 2, 9, 11, 13, 16, 18, 19, 21
Entrées
  Baked Falafel Bowl, 98–99
  Burst Cherry Tomato Rigatoni, 84
  Egg-Roll-in-a-Bowl Stir-Fry, 86
  Gnocchi Puttanesca, 91
  Hearty Chickpea Burgers, 83
  Kebabs with Spicy Peanut
    Sauce, 89–90
  Portobello Steaks with Spinach
    and Polenta, 94–95
  Potato and Leek Pie, 92
  Red Curry Vegetables, 85
  Southwest Stuffed Peppers, 82
  Spaghetti with Olive Oil,
    Garlic, and Olives, 93
  Vegan Lasagna, 87–88
  Vegetable Paella, 96–97

F

fennel, 45
  Roasted Fennel, Lentil, and
    Apple Salad, 61
Five Fast Flex Favorites, 14
  Easy Gazpacho, 78
  Egg-Roll-in-a-Bowl Stir-Fry, 86
  GLT Sandwich, 33
  Gnocchi Puttanesca, 91
  Nouveau Greek Salad, 59
  Spaghetti with Olive Oil,
    Garlic, and Olives, 93

flexitarian diet
  cooking tips, 12–13
  getting started, 8–9, 15, 18
  healthy recipes, 21
  kitchen staples, 11–12
  meal planning steps, 13
  principles of, 2
flour
  all-purpose, 17, 20
  chickpea, 17, 28
  rye, 20, 26
  whole wheat pastry, 20, 26
frozen
  fruits, 16, 19
  vegetables, 3, 11, 12, 16, 19

G

garlic
  Spaghetti with Olive Oil,
    Garlic, and Olives, 93
garlic (whole), 15, 19
garlic powder, 16, 19
ginger (fresh), 15, 19, 70, 85, 86, 116
ginger, ground, 19, 25, 26
gnocchi, 17
  Gnocchi Puttanesca, 91
grains
  Ancient Grains Salad, 56
  Carrot Cake Oatmeal, 25
  farro (pearled), 9, 11, 17, 42
  Oatmeal Hazelnut Raisin Cookies, 109
  Oatmeal-Raisin Breakfast Bowl, 24
  oats, rolled, 17
  oats, steel-cut, 20
  oats, whole, 9
  Peanut Butter Granola Bars, 103

Pear and Farro Bowl, 30
rice, Arborio, 20, 96
rice, brown, 9, 20, 82
rye berries, 56
Zucchini-Carrot Oatmeal Muffins, 27
granola, 18, 20, 31
Peanut Butter Granola Bars, 103
green beans, 15, 19, 66, 96

H

hazelnuts
Oatmeal Hazelnut Raisin Cookies, 109
heart health, 4
herbes de Provence, 16, 45

I

Italian seasoning, 16, 57

K

kale, 8
Massaged Kale Salad, 52
Plant Pesto, 113
kiwi, 8, 19, 31

L

leeks, 19
Asparagus and Leek Soup, 69
Potato and Leek Pie, 92
Potato Leek Soup, 76
lemons, 8, 16, 19
Skillet Asparagus with Lemon Zest, 41

lentils, 7, 11, 69
Roasted Fennel, Lentil, and
Apple Salad, 61
Vegetable and Lentil Stew, 72
lettuce
iceberg, 19, 33
mixed greens, 16
limes, 16, 19, 89

M

mango, 8, 19
Mango Plantain N'Ice Cream, 104
Smoothie Bowls, 3 ways, 31
maple syrup, 17, 20, 25, 26, 30,
47, 103, 104, 107, 118
Mayo Clinic, 4, 7
Measurement Conversion Charts, 121
milk
almond, unsweetened, 6, 16,
27, 30, 31, 92, 118
coconut, full fat, 17, 20, 67, 70, 85, 118
cows, 6, 117
plant-based unsweetened,
11, 19, 24, 77, 105, 107
mint, dried, 16, 59, 61, 73
miso paste, red, 17, 66
mushrooms, 8, 11, 16, 89, 112
Baked Potato with Sherried
Mushrooms, 46
cremini, 19, 70, 87
Mushroom and Scallion
Chickpea Omelet, 28
portobello, 6, 19
Portobello Steaks with Spinach
and Polenta, 94

N

nutmeg, 20, 25, 92, 117

O

oil
  canola, 86
  extra virgin olive oil, 11, 14, 17, 20
  sesame, 86
  Spaghetti with Olive Oil,
      Garlic, and Olives, 93
  vegetable, 107
olives, 8, 11
  Chopped Avocado Chickpeas
      Salad with Olives, 53
  kalamata, 17, 20
  Spaghetti with Olive Oil,
      Garlic, and Olives, 93
onion
  green, 47
  Polenta with Potato and Red Onion, 32
  red onion, 42, 53, 54, 55, 57,
      59, 60, 63, 83, 98
onion powder, 20, 43, 83
oregano, 16, 20

P

panzanella
  Panzanella Salad, 55
paprika, 17, 39, 48, 74, 83, 96, 119
parsley, dried, 17, 42, 112
parsley, flat leaf, 34, 53, 60, 74, 98
parsley, fresh, 19, 42, 54, 56, 68
parsnip, 19, 68

pasta dishes, 8, 10
  Burst Cherry Tomato Rigatoni, 84
  Gnocchi Puttanesca, 91
  Minestrone with Beans, 71
  Pearl Couscous Salad, 60
  Spaghetti with Olive Oil,
      Garlic, and Olives, 93
  Spinach Orzo Soup, 75
  Vegan Lasagna, 87
pasta sauce
  Basic Tomato Basil Sauce, 115
peaches, 8, 16, 61, 108
  Salad with Peach Carpaccio, 58
peanut butter, 17, 86
  Peanut Butter Granola Bars, 103
  Spicy Peanut Sauce, 118
pears, 16, 19, 56, 61, 108
  Apple and Pear Cake, 107
  Pear and Farro Bowl, 30
pecans, chopped, 20, 24, 25
peppers
  green bell, 15, 18, 57, 89, 96
  green chilies, diced (canned), 67
  jalapeño, 15, 17, 34, 63, 82
  orange bell, 58
  red bell, 15, 18, 29, 44, 45, 54,
      74, 78, 87, 89, 119
  Roasted Jalapeño and Lime
      Guacamole, 114
pine nuts, 7, 60, 113
pistachios, 7, 102, 113
pizza dough, 18
  Pizza Pockets, 57
plant-based diet
  benefits of, 2, 4–5
  core proteins, 7–8
  high-protein vegetables, 8

plantain
  Mango Plantain N'Ice Cream, 104
potatoes
  Baked Potato with Sherried
    Mushrooms, 46
  Cajun Sweet Potato Fries, 43
  Herb-Roasted Potatoes with Shallots, 39
  Mediterranean Potato Salad, 54
  Polenta with Potato and Red Onion, 32
  Potato Leek Soup, 76
  russet, 16, 19, 66, 68, 71, 72, 73
  sweet, 8, 19, 48, 116

Q

quinoa, 9, 11
  Quinoa Pilaf, 42

R

radishes, 16, 58
raisins, 20, 56
  Oatmeal Hazelnut Raisin Cookies, 109
  Oatmeal-Raisin Breakfast Bowl, 24
red pepper flakes, 17, 20
  Broccoli Rabe with Red Pepper Flakes, 40

S

Salads and Handhelds
  Ancient Grains Salad, 56
  Chopped Avocado Chickpea
    Salad with Olives, 53
  Family-Style Taco Bar, 63
  Mediterranean Potato Salad, 54
  Mixed Kale Salad, 52
  Nouveau Greek Salad, 59
  Panzanella Salad, 55
  Pearl Couscous Salad, 60
  Pizza Pockets, 57
  Roasted Fennel, Lentil, and
    Apple Salad, 61
  Roasted Vegetable Flatbread, 62
  Salad with Peach Carpaccio, 58
salmon, 10, 78, 90, 91
salt, 17, 20
Sauces and Staples
  Basic Tomato Basil Sauce, 115
  Hummus, 116
  Plant Pesto, 113
  Roasted Jalapeño and Lime
    Guacamole, 114
  Romesco Sauce, 119
  Spicy Peanut Sauce, 118
  Vegan Béchamel, 117
  Vegetable Broth, 112
scallions
  Mushroom and Scallion
    Chickpea Omelet, 28
seafood, 3, 10, 13, 15, 16, 21, 61, 90, 91, 97
seeds
  chia seeds, 7, 25, 31
  flaxseeds, 7, 17, 20, 26, 27, 83, 109
  pumpkin, 7, 17, 31, 102–103
  sesame, 7, 102
  sunflower, 7, 24, 52, 103
sherry, 46
shrimp, 10, 11, 16, 43, 61, 63, 85, 86, 90
slaw
  Mixed Veggie Slaw, 47
snow peas, 19, 70, 86

Soups and Stews
  Asparagus and Leek Soup, 39
  Classic Vegetable Soup, 66
  Coconut Curry Ramen, 70
  Easy Gazpacho, 78
  Minestrone with Beans, 71
  Peas and Zucchini Soup, 73
  Potato Leek Soup, 76–77
  Root Vegetable Soup, 68
  Smoky Eggplant and yellow
    Squash Soup, 74
  Spicy Corn Chowder, 67
  Spinach Orzo Soup, 75
  Vegetable and Lentil Stew, 72
spinach, 8, 11, 16, 19, 29, 31, 34, 59, 71
  Portobello Steaks with Spinach
    and Polenta, 94
  Spinach Orzo Soup, 75
squash
  Smoky Eggplant and Yellow
    Squash Soup, 74
  yellow, 16, 19, 29, 44, 89
  zucchini, 16, 19, 29, 44, 45, 84,
    87, 93 *see also* zucchini
sugar, granulated, 17, 108, 109
swiss chard, 8, 71
  Red Swiss Chard with White
    Beans, 38

T

tahini, 17, 52, 116
tempeh, 7, 86
thyme, dried, 17, 39, 42, 45, 54, 66
thyme, fresh, 19, 43, 46, 72
tofu, 7, 32, 77, 86

tomatoes, 9, 12, 14
  Basic Tomato Basil Sauce, 115
  Burst Cherry Tomato Rigatoni, 84
  cherry/grape, 16, 19, 20, 84
  crushed, canned, 11, 17, 20, 91
  diced, canned, 17, 20, 45, 71, 74, 98
tortillas, vegan, 18, 63
tuna, 10, 11, 91, 93
turnip, 8, 19, 68

V

vanilla extract, 17, 20, 26, 30, 104, 109
vegan
  butter, 19, 46, 94, 109, 117
  cheese, 16, 19, 57, 84, 87
  food prep/tips, 9, 21, 59, 77
  lifestyle, 6, 9
  Vegan Béchamel, 117
  Vegan lasagna, 87
  vegetarian type, 2
Vegetable and Sides
  Baked Potato with Sherried
    Mushrooms, 46
  Broccoli Rabe with Red
    Pepper Flakes, 440
  Cajun Sweet Potato Fries, 43
  Herb-Roasted Potatoes with Shallots, 39
  Mixed Veggie Slaw, 47
  Quinoa Pilaf, 42
  Ratatouille, 45
  Red Swiss Chard with White Beans, 38
  Roasted Mediterranean Sheet
    Pan Vegetables, 44
  Root Vegetable Chips, 48
  Skillet Asparagus with Lemon Zest, 41

vegetarian/vegan, 2
Veggie and White Bean
        Scramble, 29
vegetarian/vegan
    environmental impact, 2
vinaigrette, 14, 54, 61
vinegar
    apple cider, 53, 83
    red wine, 17, 53, 55, 59, 78
    sherry, 119
    white wine, 17, 58, 96

W

walnuts, 7, 17, 30, 42, 83
weight loss, 2
weight management, 4

wine
    white (dry), 20, 96

Y

yeast, nutritional, 18, 28, 67, 84, 113
yogurt
    coconut, 47
    Greek, 47, 59, 99

Z

zucchini
    Coconut Curry Ramen, 70
    Peas and Zucchini Soup, 73
    Zucchini-Carrot Oatmeal Muffins, 27

ACKNOWLEDGMENTS

Special thanks to my family for their love and support, especially to my brother James and sister Kathleen for testing my recipes. Thank you to Kelly Koester for guiding me through this process and for her editing advice along the way. Thank you to Matt Buonaguro for enthusiastically finding a project to match my interests and skills. I want to thank everyone at Callisto Media who worked on this book. And last but certainly not least, I'd like to thank my readers for supporting me along my food and wellness journey.

ABOUT THE AUTHOR

 **Donna DeRosa** is a journalist and food writer specializing in the Mediterranean lifestyle. She is the author of *The Big Book of Mediterranean Diet Cooking*, published by Callisto Media. She runs a self-titled YouTube channel through which she shares healthy recipes and Italian lifestyle tips. Learn more at DonnaDeRosa.com.

CPSIA information can be obtained
at www.ICGtesting.com
Printed in the USA
JSHW010037040422
24560JS00001B/2